More Than
skin deep

A Guide to Self and Soul

Crystal Kirgiss

ZONDERVAN®

ZONDERVAN.com/
AUTHORTRACKER
follow your favorite authors

We want to hear from you. Please send your comments about this book to us in care of zreview@zondervan.com. Thank you.

ZONDERVAN

More Than Skin Deep
Copyright © 2011 by Crystal Kirgiss

This title is also available as a Zondervan ebook.
Visit www.zondervan.com/ebooks.

Requests for information should be addressed to:

Zondervan, *Grand Rapids, Michigan* 49530

Library of Congress Cataloging-in-Publication Data

Kirgiss, Crystal.
       More than skin deep : a guide to self and soul / Crystal Kirgiss.
         p. cm.
       ISBN 978-0-310-66926-5 (softcover : alk. paper)
         1. Teenage girls—Religious life. 2 Christian teenagers—Religious life. I. Title.
     BV4551.3.K56 2011
     248.8'33—dc22   2011014463

Cover design: Micah Kandros Design
Cover photography : micahkandrosphotography.com
Interior design: Ben Fetterley & Greg Johnson/Textbook Perfect

Printed in the United States of America

11 12 13 14 15 16 /DCI/ 22 21 20 19 18 17 16 15 14 13 12 11 10 9 8 7 6 5 4 3 2 1

More Than
skin
deep

Other books by Crystal Kirgiss:

What's Up with Boys?:
Everything You Need to Know about Guys

Creative Bible Lessons on the Prophets: 12 Sessions Packed with
Ancient Truth for the Present

With Pam Stenzel:

Sex Has a Price Tag: Discussions about Sexuality,
Spirituality, and Self-Respect

With Helen Musick and Dan Jessup:

Girls: 10 Gutsy, God-Centered Sessions
on Issues That Matter to Girls

Guys: 10 Fearless, Faith-Focused Sessions
on Issues That Matter to Guys

Acknowledgements

Many people help give birth to a book. These are just a few of the many who helped deliver this one, safe and sound:

Aliya, Amy, Bryssa, Cassidy, Eden, Emma, Evelyn, Katrina, Lauryn, Sage (and their mothers)

Kenny Sipes, Becky Wellner, Mark Kirgiss, Carly Roach (and a bunch of other youth leaders)

Brooke Hilsmeyer, Amy Taylor, Ruby Behringer, Annie Surber, Amanda Sliepka, Brittany Atkinson, Emi Reinebold, and Kristin Parry (and a hundred other college women)

Melodie Stewart, Molly Gephart, Sarah Bowker, Nancy Homan, Jessica Wade, Nicole Smith, Paige Homeier, Jessie Behr, Jordan Hainje, Megan Posas, Katie Carlson, Maddi Miller, Linnea Miller, Abby Davis, Rylie Sanders, Zhanna Makarova, Abby Springs, Miranda Nelson, Lexy Madrid, Jessica Gibson, Victoria Lovelace, Monica Foutty, Leah Davis, Julia Newton, Hannah Wolf, Laurie Jones, Alexa Hershey, Ashley McCord, Taylor Conley, Jerrica Assadian, Katie O'Neill, Emily Beckman, Mekenzie Hilsmeyer, Annie Kramer (and a thousand other high school girls)

And (especially) my husband, who puts up with a lot when I'm writing; and my sons, who I've never once wished were girls instead.

chapter
1

Skin versus skin

JUNIOR HIGH WASN'T MY FAVORITE TIME OF LIFE. BECAUSE OF BIZARRE district boundary lines, I'd gone to an elementary school on the west side of town but then got assigned to the junior high on the east side of town. All of my elementary school friends went to the west side junior high. The new junior high. The awesome junior high. The junior high with a full-size gym and a legit cafeteria. The junior high with carpeted hallways, bright windows, and huge classrooms.

But not me.

Instead of walking out of my neighborhood and turning right, like I'd done for the past however-many years of my life, I now turned left — east — and walked into the great unknown. For some people, this might not have been an issue. For someone like me, who didn't have an overabundance of friends and who wasn't overly outgoing, it was a tragic moment of epic proportions. I headed east that first day with faint hopes of building a new life for myself, convinced that things couldn't get any worse than they already were.

Wrong.

Kids from three different elementary schools attended my junior high, so in theory the students knew only one-third of their new class-mates and were strangers to the other two-thirds. In that sense, my situation as the new kid wasn't totally hopeless. But instead of getting placed in a typical homeroom where students knew only one-third of their new classmates and were strangers to the other two-thirds (decent odds for the new girl), I got placed in a section with twenty-or-so stu-dents who'd all been each others' classmates for the last two years and each others' schoolmates for the four years before that (they were in some experimental program for Talented and Gifted Students) and were *all* on a first-name basis with *everyone*. They had inside jokes. They had nicknames for each other . . . *nice* nicknames. Nicknames of endear-ment. They knew each other's parents and siblings. They were — or at least it seemed to me — a family. And I was the stranger. The new girl. The outsider.

Fantastic. Marvelous. Lucky me.

I'd been in a similar situation in second grade when my family had moved to the other side of the suburbs halfway through the school year. I'd gotten a new home, new neighbors, new school, new teacher, new classmates, new *everything*, and it was kind of scary . . . for about ten minutes. I'd walked into my new second-grade classroom — where every-one already knew everyone else, and everyone already had a desk, and everyone already had friends, and everyone already knew the rules and the routines, and everyone already had art projects hanging on the wall — and held my breath in panic for about three minutes, at which point a girl named Cynthia came up to me and said, "Wanna see what I'm learning how to make?" and my world was okay again. It was as easy as that. But things sometimes aren't as easy in junior high as in second grade.

For me, starting at a new school wasn't as easy the second time around, because I didn't have quite as much self-confidence — and I had a lot more self-consciousness — when I walked into my new junior high as when I'd walked into my new elementary school almost five years earlier. For starters, I was aware of Boys (with a capital B). Up to that point, they'd just been boys — lowercase b — neither greater than nor less than girls. But now, well, they were still neither greater than nor less than girls, but they certainly were very different than us. I wasn't necessarily interested in them as Boys, if you know what I mean — but there were plenty of girls who were interested in them as Boys, and that was a whole new world of drama and romance and gossip that I wasn't ready for. Still, my intense awareness of them made me act differently. Sometimes silly, sometimes stupid, sometimes awkward, sometimes aloof.

On top of that, I was sure that every person passing me in the hall was thinking, "New girl. Bad skin. Look out." A year earlier, I'd had two skin-related episodes that were more than mildly distressing. First, I'd gotten pimples. Zits. Acne. Whatever. I didn't care what they were called, I only cared that I had them and my friends didn't. How unfair could life be? Pretty unfair, it turns out, because just a few months after getting pimples, I got chicken pox. For two long weeks, I watched pox multiply among all the other imperfections on my face, prohibited by the doctor from scrubbing for fear of making everything worse, which was small comfort because when the chicken pox were gone, the scars and the pimples were still there. When I finally went back to school, one girl came up to me in the lunch line and said, "Gee, it's kind of hard to tell that you don't have chicken pox anymore because your face looks so awful anyway."

How do you reply to that? I just turned away and kept filling my lunch tray.

On that first day of seventh grade, I still had bad skin. (Why do you suppose we call it bad, as though it has its own will and is guilty of misbehaving or being disobedient? It's not as though my skin had any choice in the matter.) And I still thought it was unfair because so many other people had good skin. Even perfect skin. Why was I one of the unlucky ones? Oh well. At least I had my health. (That's what grandmas and great-aunts say to make us feel better, but it's not at all helpful or comforting.)

Truthfully my complexion issues didn't totally drag me down. I actually felt pretty good about myself in some ways. I was a good student. I could play piano well. I liked my family. And I was determined to make some new friends in my new school — friends who I could hang out with for the next few years, friends who would like me for who I was.

Then came Second Hour — social studies. We had to read a short chapter about I-don't-remember-what, and then the teacher started asking us questions about what we'd read. I prayed she would skip me. After all, I was the new girl. I didn't know anyone. I was from the west side of town. I had bad skin. Surely she would sense my discomfort and unease and move on to the next student.

Wrong.

She ignored all my mental commands to "Skip me! Ignore me! Don't notice me!" and asked me what I thought about question number three. I withered. I froze. I panicked. I wept (inwardly, of course). And then I thought, *This is my opportunity to show that I'm confident. That I'm intelligent. That I'm not afraid of a challenge. That I can be a strong person who would be a good — no, a great friend — to anyone. That I'm not a cowardly, bumbling, introverted nobody. That I am somebody.* So I cleared my throat and delivered what I thought was an amazing and stellar answer.

As soon as I finished, a boy near the back of the room snickered and said sarcastically, "That is the stupidest thing I've ever heard."

Crisis. What should I do? What should I say? I didn't know anyone, so I wasn't sure if he was the class clown I should ignore (with a condescending "hmmmmph") or the class leader I should try to impress (with my own sarcastic comment). I didn't know if I should respond directly, or pretend I hadn't heard. I didn't know whether to shrug it off, or rise to the challenge. I was totally frozen.

But I knew my answer hadn't been stupid. I knew *I* wasn't stupid. And I knew I deserved better than being ridiculed and mocked on my first day in a new school.

So from the front of the room, with everyone looking to see what I'd do, I stared that boy straight in the eye, took a deep breath, and said, "You're wrong. My answer was good. Really good."

Silence.

Total and complete silence.

The teacher, who was super old, seemed unaware of what was going on. But the students all knew exactly what had happened. There'd been a stand-off between the New Girl and One of the Guys (who, it turns out, was neither the class clown nor the class leader). I held my breath. The boy in back held his breath. Time stood still. And then the boy in the back slouched down in his desk, rolled his eyes, and said, "You are so stuck-up."

Stuck-up?! Me?! Was he kidding?! If he'd had any idea of how nervous I was about being the new girl ... if he'd had even an inkling of how self-conscious I was about my complexion ... if he'd had even the remotest sense of how worried I was about making new friends in a new school ... then he would have known I was anything but stuck-up. I was so shocked by his comment that I couldn't reply. I went back to my seat. Sat down. Blushed. Hid my disappointment and worry and fear. Tried to hold my head up high and not be defeated.

By lunch time that day, I was known as "Stucky" to everyone in my class, a nickname that stuck through all of junior high.

I hated my life.

"Love the Skin You're In"

That's a popular catchphrase in today's world. Do an Internet search, and you'll get more than sixty-eight million hits for the phrase. That's right. Sixty-eight *million*. And all the sites are about (no big surprise) skin. Real skin. The stuff that covers your bones and muscles and veins and tendons and organs and other gross, gooey stuff. Some of the sites are about makeup. Some are about moisturizers. Some are about tanning salons. Some are about beauty salons. Some are about body shape. Some are about body size. Some are about anti-aging products. Some are about beauty products. Some are about freckles. Some are about pimples. They're all about skin. Literal, physical skin.

Now, this book isn't about physical skin — the pigmented, freckled, soft, calloused, tanned, wrinkled, smooth, mosquito-bitten, spider-veined, porous, rug-burned, pierced, delicate, strong bodycovering that holds you all together. This book is about a different kind of skin.

The skin we're talking about is *you*. Your own self. Your own identity. Your own uniqueness. Your own who-you-are-ness. You. That's right. *You* are the subject, topic, and star of this book.

Don't get me wrong. Your biological skin, which holds together all the gazillion amazing parts of your body, is truly one of God's most amazing creations. Here's some skin trivia:

- Skin is the body's largest organ. The average surface area is between fourteen and eighteen square feet.
- On average, humans shed six hundred thousand particles of skin every hour — 1.5 pounds of skin a year.
- Each square inch of skin contains nineteen million cells, sixty hairs, ninety oil glands, twenty feet of blood vessels, six hundred twenty-five sweat glands, nineteen thousand sensory cells, and millions of bacteria.

- Each person's skin is renewed every twenty-eight days. That's about one thousand new skins per lifetime.

Each time I get a mosquito bite or a cut or a burn that eventually heals itself, I realize how miraculous and wondrous skin is. But we're not going to talk about it much in this book because there are lots of other places where you can get advice on skin care. The skin we're going to talk about — let's call it Skin with a capital *S* — is the thing that holds all your invisible pieces together: your passions, thoughts, identity, ideas, dreams, hopes, values, beliefs, joys, fears, sorrows, and so much more.

Some people believe girls are defined by their skin (color and condition) and what it covers (shape and size). But they're wrong. The truth is, girls are defined by their Skin (grace and kindness) and what it covers (see the long list above). Unfortunately, the magazines, TV shows, movies, Internet sites, radio stations, and advice books don't pay much attention to Skin.

Sure, they might talk about it here and there, now and then, once in a while. (That is, they throw in a token, one-page article on "serving your community" or "getting along with your parents" or "being kind to strangers" or "discovering your passions.") But Skin isn't their main focus nor their area of expertise. They care about skin. Plain and simple. The exterior biological shell. Christians care about skin, too, because God created it and it allows us to be God's hands and feet on earth. But Christians care (or at least they *should* care) way more about Skin.

So I guess you could say this book is about "Skin care" as opposed to "skin care," something I wish I'd known more about in junior high.

Skin care is especially important for girls in junior high and high school because something happens during those years that causes a Skin crisis. The crisis might last for a week, or for years. It might be slightly uncomfortable, or deeply painful. It might be somewhat troublesome, or seriously tragic. It's different for every girl. But sometime, somewhere, for some reason, almost every girl finds herself wondering, *Who am I? What's going on? Why do I feel so uncomfortable and awkward? Why can't I be more like her? Or her? Or even her? What's my problem? Why don't I feel happy? Why do they think I'm stuck-up? What's wrong with me, anyway?!*

Another way to think about the crisis is this: It's the moment when a girl starts feeling uncomfortable in her own skin. And her own Skin. Often, it starts with outer appearance — something skin deep — like height, weight, shape, hair color, or skin type. But then it moves into something deeper — something Skin deep — and she starts wishing she were someone else completely, someone with a different personality, different characteristics, different feelings and thoughts and emotions. Sometimes how we feel about our skin affects how we feel about our Skin, and we waste hours and weeks and years thinking that if we could just change our skin, then our Skin would be different too, and life would be perfect and happy and fabulous.

That's what the world wants us to believe, anyway.

The Skin Crisis

One time when I was hanging out with my best friend, her six-year-old daughter came dancing into the room, twirling and spinning, lunging and leaping, smiling and giggling, full of joy and energy and laughter. She paused for a moment, looked at her silhouette reflected in the picture window, curtsied, performed an elaborate and elegant twirl, then continued on through the room, a whirlwind of little-girl confidence and contentment.

My friend smiled and sighed, then said, "I wish I could bottle up all that confidence and joy and save it for a day when she's going to need it."

I knew exactly what she was talking about.

The Skin crisis.

Something that every girl experiences.

The world — the magazines, TV shows, movies, music, celebrities, chat sites, experts, and more — wants you to think they really care about, and know about, Skin care. But if you listen and watch and read carefully, you'll see their questions and answers almost always focus on something shallow, commercial, short-term. Are you unhappy at school? Get a new pair of shoes! Are you having trouble with your friends? Buy this brand of jeans! Are you tired of your parents? Go out with a new guy! Are you struggling with feelings of stress and sadness? Try some new perfume! Are you trying to figure out who you are and how you fit into the world around you? Dye your hair a new color! Are you feeling lonely and left out? A new totebag and pair of sunglasses will fix things!

And so it goes, on and on.

Recently, I made some calculations of the contents in a teen magazine. Of the advertisements:

- 30 percent were for shoes
- 25 percent were for hair-removal, skin-care, and hair-care products
- 20 percent were for designer clothes
- 19 percent were for accessories (especially sunglasses and purses)
- 6 percent were for perfume, private schools, tampons, bottled water, milk, and other things

In the photo layouts of models, there were another eighty-eight ads for accessories, seventy-two for designer clothes, and twenty-nine for shoes.

The articles were about diets, tanning, romantic relationships, dating abuse, and celebrities. There was also a horoscope and an advice column, both of which focused heavily on sex and dating. Wow.

This is what I believe: A lot of our culture's magazines (and movies, songs, and websites) are full of blah-blah nonsense. That's right.

BLAH-BLAH, STUPID, UNTRUE, RIDICULOUS, GIVE-ME-A-BREAK, YOU'VE-GOT-TO-BE-KIDDING, NONSENSE! Most of what they offer and show and say is, well, dumb, if you really take the time to think about it. How is another pair of shoes going to make life better? How is looking sexy in a bathing suit going to give your life meaning and purpose? How is a new belt or bracelet or boy going to make you someone different than you really are?

Our culture asks the wrong questions — Is he into you? What bathing suit is best for your body type? What style of jeans will make you look thinner? — and so it gives the wrong answers.

Plus, our culture doesn't understand Skin. Skin is God's specialty. God is the only one who really knows what's going on inside of you, who really understands you, and who really knows what you need for a full and fantastic life. Unfortunately, you can't pick up the newest issue of God at the newsstand, or download him onto your phone for free, or get him as a pay-per-view special. God's not available in a glossy, high-def, downloadable format.

But then, neither are you. And that's why our culture's answers won't ever help you understand or get through a Skin crisis.

The situation is much deeper than that. It's more than skin deep. It's Skin deep.

So in the chapters that follow, we're going to talk about Skin. And unlike the world's idea to merely "love the skin you're in," we're going to talk about how to "celebrate the Skin you're in." It's not that you shouldn't love something God created (you). You *should* love yourself (and your neighbor just as much, and God even more). But it's got to go further than that. If you just love yourself, and that love doesn't make a difference, or doesn't get shared with the other people in your life, or doesn't affect the world around you in a positive way, then what's the point? That's why this book is about celebrating (accepting, loving, and

chapter
2

Skin Crisis, Part I

LIFE IS A STRANGE MIX OF GOOD AND BAD, ISN'T IT? EVEN WHEN things are going great — you and your friends are getting along, things are good at home, you aced a test, you made the varsity team, you got the part-time job, you got a "superior" at band contest — there are usually at least one or two things that aren't exactly perfect or the way you'd like them. On the other hand, even when things are totally awful — your friends have abandoned you, your mom is on your case about everything, you failed your physics test (again), you got moved down to junior varsity, you got a "no thanks" on your job application, you got a "fair" at band contest — there are usually at least one or two bright spots in your day that make you smile and feel okay about life.

Life is never totally great or totally awful. It's always a mix of the two. Of course, people can choose whether to focus on the good or the bad — and people who focus on the good tend to be happier, more content, and more fun to be around. But sometimes the bad is pretty

re, in your face, following you down the
y minute of every day.

ght in the crossfire of this strange combination.
ke the good and bad are going at each other so
at it's impossible to escape the chaos they cause.
so many girls complain about the drama in their lives.
Drama isn't just for teenage girls. Middle-aged people
Old people have drama. Children have drama. Here's what
ig girls said when asked what the best and worst things were
eing a girl:

The best thing about being a girl is that I have a pink princess bath-
suit. The worst thing about being a girl is that I have to wait until
Daddy gets home to go swimming." (Evelyn, age three)

"The best thing about being a girl is that I get to play with dolls and wear dresses. The worst thing about being a girl is having to do work I don't want to, like cleaning up." (Aliya, age five)

"The best thing about being a girl is having long hair. The worst thing about being a girl is having a small room, like mine." (Amy, age six)

"The best thing about being a girl is that I can have long hair that blows in the wind when I swing. The worst part about being a girl is combing my hair." (Emma, age seven)

"The best thing about being a girl is that I'm smart. The worst thing about being a girl is trying to take care of siblings." (Cassidy, age eight)

"The best thing about being a girl is going shopping with my mom. The worst thing about being a girl is being told I can't do some things because I'm a girl." (Lauryn, age nine)

"The best thing about being a girl is having girlfriends. The worst part about being a girl is when your girlfriends try to make you feel bad." (Katrina, age nine)

Skin crises have been around for a long time—they're not just a twenty-first century phenomena. I have a collection of old books for girls that talk about many of the same things this book does. The wording is a little stuffier and the fashions are outdated, but the topics are similar. You can tell just by looking at some of the titles:

Strictly Confidential (1944)
Beautiful Girlhood (1922)
Girlhood and Character (1916)
What A Young Woman Ought to Know (1898)
Personal Beauty (1870)

You'll find some quotes from these old books scattered throughout this new book. Some are obviously outdated (like the one telling girls how many baths—yes, *baths!*—to take each week), while others are still true. When you read them, remember that girls have been facing many of the same issues and Skin crises for a long, long time.

"The best thing about being a girl is that we can do both boy and girl things, and we can have babies. The worst thing about being a girl is that we always have to keep our shirts on, and going to the bathroom is way more complicated." (Eden, age ten)

"The best thing about being a girl is that you have friends you can trust with your secrets, ideas, and other important girl stuff. The worst part about being a girl is that some people don't keep your secrets, ideas, and other important girl stuff. Instead they tell the whole school . . . even if you thought they were your best friends." (Bryssa, age ten)

"The best thing about being a girl is that we can be anything we want to be, but boys would be teased if they took ballet or fashion class. The worst part about being a girl is that we're not always accepted by boys." (Sage, age twelve)

Obviously this mix of good and bad stuff starts long before the teen years. Even young girls who come from good homes, have loving parents, and are lucky enough to own pink princess bathing suits have to deal with both good and bad stuff. But for some reason, when you're a teenager, this mix somehow seems so much more dramatic, doesn't it? I'll bet many of you would be happy if the worst thing in your life was having to clean up your toys, or having to comb tangly hair, or having to deal with pesty siblings. I'm not saying those crises aren't real — they are. But the crises that many teen girls face seem huge in comparison.

Why? Because so many of them are Skin deep; they affect us at our inner core, our most personal self, and our very identity.

I've talked to tons of teen girls about the Skin crisis, that thing we talked about in chapter one. They all agreed that it's very real. They all agreed that for each of them, it started somewhere in junior or senior high. They all agreed that it's hard to pinpoint exactly what caused it and that it's pretty awful sometimes. They all agreed that they haven't quite figured out how to deal with it and that they'd like some help surviving it.

That's the goal for the rest of this book.

Before we go any further, take a few minutes and answer these two questions. Don't look ahead to see how others responded — just write your own, honest answers.

What's the best thing about being a girl?

What's the worst thing about being a girl?

Here's how some teen girls answered the same questions. See if any of these sound familiar:

The best thing about being a girl is:

- There is always something to talk about (age fifteen)
- Being able to show emotion without society frowning upon it (age fifteen)
- Multitasking (age fifteen)
- Developing close, deep relationships with other girls (age seventeen)
- Getting dressed up (age seventeen)
- Someday getting to have children (age fifteen)
- Being in touch with our emotions (age sixteen)
- Clothes! (age sixteen)
- Girls Night (age eighteen)
- Funky nailpolish colors (age thirteen)
- Lower rates for car insurance (age fifteen)
- High heels (age seventeen)
- Natural shopping ability (age eighteen)
- I just love being a girl! (age thirteen)

The worst or hardest thing about being a girl is:

- The drama that some of my friends think they need to be involved in (age fourteen)
- Constantly being judged on every part of your life (age fifteen)
- Learning how to love yourself despite the overwhelming feeling that you must look or be a certain way (age fifteen)
- PMS, gossip, and drama (age fifteen)
- Little brothers (age thirteen)
- Understanding my emotions (age fourteen)
- Not being pretty or skinny enough (age fourteen)

- Acting ladylike (age fourteen)
- Having too much confidence can lead to becoming bossy ... and no one likes someone who's bossy (age fifteen)
- Cramps (age sixteen)
- Drama! (age eighteen)
- That time of the month (age seventeen)
- Cliques! (age sixteen)
- Pressure to fit in by being skinny (age fifteen)
- Trying to find modest clothes (age eighteen)
- Rumors, gossip, and lies (age sixteen)
- Shaving (age seventeen)
- Having to spend so much time on appearance (age sixteen)
- The emotional distress of it all (age sixteen)

In all of the surveys, the top answers for the best thing about being a girl were:

- Having close friendships
- Dressing up
- Being in touch with emotions
- Getting to have children someday
- Multitasking

The top answers for the hardest part about being a girl were:

- Gossip
- PMS
- Drama
- Emotions
- Pressure to be thin and pretty

Here's the deal — the Skin crisis every girl faces is partly biological, a result of being female. That's why so many of the answers from different-aged girls (who are from different places — small town, big city,

Midwest, East Coast, West Coast, etc.) are similar. A few years ago I wrote a book about guys, and when I asked guys the question, "What's the hardest part about being a guy?" the answers were very different from the girls' answers you just read. Obviously PMS wasn't on any of their lists except in a few cases where guys said, "The hardest part about being a guy is dealing with my sister's PMS." Gossip, drama, and backstabbing friends weren't on any lists, either. The crises that guys dealt with had more to do with feelings of being a loser, worries about not being strong and tough enough, and confusion about understanding girls. It looks as though gossip, PMS (obviously), drama, emotions, and pressure to be thin and pretty are *uniquely girl issues.* And they all, in their own way, impact a girl's Skin crisis.

Before going any further, let's be clear about a few things: First, every girl is different from every other girl. Second, every Skin crisis is different from every other Skin crisis. Third, guys are not completely different or totally opposite from girls. There are lots of false stereotypes about both guys and girls that can lead to a lot of confusion and pain (for both guys and girls).

But on the other hand ... there are also some differences between guys and girls that are very well documented by doctors and scientists, and *some* of those differences might have *something* to do with the Skin crisis that *some* girls face.

Gossip

Did you know that on average, girls speak three times more words each day than guys? Most girls are language experts. Word masters. Conversation queens. And since gossip involves talking, well, it's not difficult to see why gossip is an issue for some girls. Certainly, not all girls gossip. And the girls from the survey who said that gossip is one of the worst things about being a girl probably weren't talking about themselves when they gossip — instead they probably were talking about when they've been the one being gossiped about. We all know that's one of the most painful experiences in life.

Maybe another reason gossip is such an issue for some girls is because girls are usually taught that it's "not ladylike" to hit, punch, fight, or attack another girl. Of course some girls do get into physical fights, but for the most part, if girls want to inflict pain on each other, their weapons of choice are words.

And by the way, the old nursery rhyme, "Sticks and stones can break my bones, but names can never hurt me," isn't entirely true. Words may not damage a person's skin the same way the sticks and stones can, but they certainly can damage a person's Skin. And I'm not talking about a silly junior-high nickname like "Stucky"; I'm talking about horrid, hurtful names that classmates, peers, and even family members call some girls. I won't list them here — they're too awful. But if you've ever been on the receiving end of one of those names, you know what I'm talking about. And if you've ever called another girl one of those names, may I suggest that you gather up all the courage and humility you can and offer her a face-to-face apology. She deserves it.

PMS

This answer came up over and over again, in all kinds of different forms. *PMS. Cramps. Raging hormones. That time of the month. The monthly visitor. My little friend.* You can add your own phrase to the list. First off, PMS is different for every girl, so don't assume that your experience is the same as someone else's. Secondly, PMS is very real, but it's also very mysterious. Doctors have all kinds of theories about what causes it, but in the end, they're all just theories.

Basically, girls have two major hormones — estrogen and progesterone. Throughout the month, these hormones have fluctuating levels,

"This change in the body is so rapid, and it affects the disposition so greatly, that the girl gets all out of harmony with herself ... It is her same body, she is herself, but for reasons that she cannot fathom everything seems different." (from *Beautiful Girlhood*, 1922)

which is totally normal. (The major hormone for guys is testosterone, and its levels fluctuate daily instead of monthly.) When levels of estrogen and progesterone fluctuate, there are both physical and emotional symptoms. The most obvious physical effect is that you have a period (or a "menstrual cycle," for those of you taking health class right now). And quite possibly cramps. For some girls it's no big deal. For other girls it's a pretty serious thing that requires a doctor's intervention. Hormones also affect the brain, and that's why some girls — both before and during their periods — may find themselves reacting and responding to things more strongly than usual. Some girls find themselves getting angry easily or being sad at the slightest thing or feeling irritable about stuff that doesn't usually bother them. A lot of this could be due to fluctuating hormone levels.

If a girl is having a really hard time with PMS, it's never fair (or wise) to say, "She's totally PMSing," or, "She's got raging hormones." That reduces a very real and genuine experience to something meaningless and shallow. On the other hand, it's never okay to excuse your own bad behavior by saying, "It's PMS, get off my case." If you're feeling out of control or inexplicably unhappy or extremely irritable, and if it's affecting how you treat other people (especially your family members), then you need to talk to someone about ways to alleviate the symptoms and the situation.

One more thing before moving on: Almost every single girl I've ever known or talked to about this issue absolutely *hates* having periods. They believe it's unfair. They believe it's rotten. They say it ruins their lives. They'd give anything (they say) to *not* have to deal with periods.

Fair enough. Periods *can* be an inconvenience. They *can* be nuisances. They *can* be uncomfortable and even painful. (But just think about what it was like for your grandmas and great-grandmas and great-great-great-grandmas, before the days of disposable products, when they had to use cloth pads that had to be laundered and reused!) I understand and empathize with all of the complaints I hear from girls about this issue.

But ... I want you to try thinking about it in a different way: Every time you have your period, instead of considering it a crisis, consider it a miracle. I know — that sounds crazy! But hang on a sec. When you were born, even *before* you were born, you carried inside your body about three hundred single-celled eggs, each with the potential to become a living, breathing baby. Your body was created by God with the ability to carry new life. And each time you have a period, it's a reminder of this amazing, miraculous fact. *Remember: You are a female. You are the bearer of life. You are indescribably, fantastically, wondrously, miraculously made!*

Drama & Emotions

These two responses often go hand in hand, so let's talk about them together. They're not quite as biologically concrete as PMS, but here are a few reasons why girls are more apt to get emotionally sucked into (or to create) drama. This has to do with how a female brain works. In recent years, brain researchers have conducted all kinds of studies, and they've learned some amazing things about how the human brain functions in certain situations most of the time. (Of course, there are always exceptions, and there's a range of behavior — all girls' brains don't function exactly the same.)

For instance, this probably comes as no surprise, but girls tend to analyze certain things — such as facial expressions, conversations, relationships, and emotions — more than guys do. Here's how the neurological theory goes (and there are lots of studies and CAT scans to back this up): Brains have three layers. While emotions originate in the middle layer for both sexes, they're usually processed in the lower layer in guys' brains, which is sometimes called the "flight or fight" center of the brain. (You can read more about this in *What's Up with Boys?*) But in girls' brains, emotions are usually processed in the top layer of the brain — the thinking and analyzing center. Therefore girls tend to take an emotion (or something they've seen or something they've heard) and look at it from every possible angle. Then they might turn it over in their brains, break it apart, and look at it *again* from every possible angle. Then they might talk about it with friends, worry about it, think about it, even obsess about it, and repeat the process again ... and maybe again and again and again.

If the neurologists are correct, it's easy to see how drama and emotions are an issue for lots of girls. If you've ever found yourself wondering, "Why did she look at me like that? Is she mad at me? Did I do something wrong? Did I say something wrong? Is she going to talk about me behind my back? What has she said about me? I'll bet she hates me. I'll bet she's going to lie about me to my friends. I'll bet she already *has* lied about me to my friends! She always did hate me," (and so on and so on) you know what I'm talking about. Even the most self-controlled and even-tempered girls can find themselves in one of these emotional-drama tangles. Some find themselves driven and controlled by all of the mental and emotional gymnastics taking place in their brains. It's easy to see why so many girls list "drama" and "emotions" as some of the worst things about being a girl. It can be exhausting, terrifying, maddening, consuming, and terribly sad. (Don't forget, though: Because girls spend so much time analyzing their own emotions, they're often very in tune with how other people are feeling, and that's probably one of the reasons why "deep friendships" rank high on the list of *best* things about being a girl.)

Pressure to be Thin and Pretty

This issue came up in almost every single survey and conversation I had for this book. Even the most slender, beautiful girls said they felt pressure to be thinner and prettier than they already were. The pressure to look a certain way has always existed for women. In the Old Testament book of Esther, young women primped and preened for months in the hopes that they'd be chosen as the next queen. It doesn't matter that their fashions and hairstyles were different than today's — there was still pressure to look a certain way and be a certain shape or size.

Today the pressure is magnified a million times over because we're constantly bombarded with images of what our culture considers the perfect female. She's slim, has fabulously thick and shiny hair, high cheekbones, full lips, arched eyebrows, curves in all the right places, long eyelashes, and an amazing wardrobe. (Of course she doesn't really exist. She's an airbrushed, artist-enhanced, media-created illusion. But that doesn't make it any easier to deal with the pressure to be like her.)

Every single female I know has at least one physical attribute she'd like to change. No girl is totally happy with how she looks. I was amazed at some of the responses I got from girls when asked what they wished were different about their appearances: *Taller. Thinner. Straight hair. Curly hair. Smaller knees. Smaller ears. Smaller feet. Smaller thighs. Bigger chest. Smaller chest. Smaller hips. Smaller this. Bigger that.*

For some girls the dissatisfaction is only skin deep — they don't like their hair (knees/thighs/ears/whatever), but they're still fairly content with who they are. But for other girls the dissatisfaction goes beyond skin deep to Skin deep. Their unhappiness with their physical appearance (skin) grows into dissatisfaction with their inner selves (Skin), and they judge their Skin with the same critical lens that they judge their skin.

This is one of the saddest and most unfortunate situations for any girl. One of the most devastating lies in the world is that skin (outer appearance) must look a certain way in order for a girl to be beautiful. Another equally devastating lie is that skin defines Skin. Fortunately the Bible is clear that skin and Skin — though both integral parts of a person — do not define one another, and that Skin, not skin, is what really matters. Even so, many girls find that a skin crisis leads to a Skin crisis.

But there are other things besides a skin crisis that can lead to a Skin crisis. That's what we'll talk about in the next chapter.

Going More than Skin Deep:

1. Think back to one of the first times you started feeling unhappy about your skin and/or Skin. What were the circumstances? How did you respond?
2. Why do you suppose so many girls are so susceptible to our culture's pressures to look a certain way? Is there anything you can do to lessen that pressure (for yourself and others)?
3. How would you describe your Skin to someone?

chapter
3

Skin Crisis, Part II

IN JUNIOR AND SENIOR HIGH, I WAS UNHAPPY WITH MY APPEARANCE for lots of reasons:

1. Thin, baby-fine hair that wouldn't hold a curl, no matter what I did
2. High, receding forehead that made me look like George Washington if I pulled back my hair into a ponytail
3. A five-foot two-inch frame (on a tall day) that was almost always the shortest in the class
4. Skin that was liberally covered with a variety of blemishes
5. Pale, Scandinavian skin that would only burn, not tan, no matter what
6. A face that was round, round, round, round, round (Did I mention *round*?)
7. A pointy, jutted chin (George Washington all over again)
8. A crooked and uneven smile that *never* looked good in pictures
9. A waist-to-hip ratio that didn't fit any brand or style of jeans
10. A prominent, bumped nose

You get the idea.

I look at this list now and am appalled that I cared so much about things that didn't — and still don't — matter, and that I didn't — and still don't — have any control over. Such is how many teen girls and young women judge themselves.

I don't know why those things were so important to me back then. I should've known better. I loved Jesus, and I knew he loved me. I knew God created me and that "God doesn't make any junk" (a popular phrase back then that was supposed to make all of us teen girls feel better about ourselves — didn't work so well). I knew that outer appearance was superficial and fleeting and that inner beauty and character were what counted. I knew that being hung up about hair and skin and height and weight led to shallow vanity and pride. I knew I had value and worth just as I was.

But I still really, really wished I had thicker hair, darker eyelashes, a thinner face, and a gorgeous smile.

For some reason, despite all of my confidence (and I did have some because I really believed that I mattered and had value) and all of my deep faith in God's love for me, I still fell prey to the culture's message about the importance of outer beauty. I had a skin crisis. But I also had a Skin crisis. I wasn't just dissatisfied with my outer appearance — there were other things I wanted to change.

I wanted to be funnier.

I wanted to be more outgoing.

I wanted to know what to say to people when they asked me questions about Jesus.

I wanted to be less of a loner.

I wanted to have a bubbly personality that attracted people.

I wanted to be a good singer.

I wanted to be athletic.

I wanted to be a leader.

I wanted, I wanted, I wanted . . .

My own Skin crisis was worse than some people's, and not as bad as other people's. I guess I had what you'd call an average Skin crisis. And in fact, feeling average was a major part of the problem. I hated being average. (It was just so . . . *average*.) Most of us want to be above-average or best at something, but really the only thing we can definitely be best at is being ourselves, which isn't to say that it's bad to try and be the best student, best swimmer, best singer, best whatever . . . but when we judge the value of our Skin by whether or not we're best at something, well, we're just setting ourselves up for disappointment.

I don't know exactly what your Skin crisis is like, but I can guess that it probably has something to do with appearance, personality traits, or friends, like most Skin crises. But just like there are unique things about your Skin, there are also unique things about your Skin crisis — things that only you know. When most girls describe or talk about their Skin crises, they first talk about things they'd like to change, or things they wish were different about them. So for starters I want you to make a list here of all the things you'd like to change about yourself — inner, outer, whatever.

I'm not suggesting that focusing on things we're unhappy about, or things we'd like to change, is a good way to spend our time — but it's a good place to start in terms of figuring out just what's at the root of a Skin crisis.

Things I Wish I Could Change:

Things Young Girls Wish They Could Change:

"I wish I could have my own room." (Cassidy, age seven)

"I wish I could change my hair ... no ... I would just keep it the same." (Aliya, age five)

"I wish I was the same age as my friend, Lauren." (Katrina, age nine)

"I wish I had better drawing skills." (Emma, age seven)

"I wish I had long hair." (Amy, age six)

"I wish my dad would come home so I could go swimming." (Evelyn, age three)

"I wish I could change my emotions." (Lauryn, age nine)

"I wish I could change the way I react to things." (Bryssa, age ten)

"I wish I could fly and write faster." (Eden, age ten)

"I wish I could be good at everything ... sports, math, everything else!" (Sage, age twelve)

Here's what some girls your age would like to change about themselves:

"I wish I could obey Jesus without chickening out." (age fourteen)

"I wish I were more open with people." (age fourteen)

"I wish I were taller, nicer, and closer to God." (age fourteen)

"I wish I wasn't always the strong one. Sometimes you just need to cry and I can't." (age fifteen)

"I wish I were more outgoing." (age thirteen)

"I wish I knew what to say at certain times ... or that I didn't say anything at other times." (age fourteen)

"I wish I felt more secure about myself." (age sixteen)

"I wish I could change my attitude." (age eighteen)

"I wish my thighs were just a tiny bit smaller ... and that I would realize what I'm saying or doing before I actually do it."
(age seventeen)

"I wish it were easier for me to jump right into new groups and conversations." (age seventeen)

"I wish I could lose twenty pounds ... and not be so annoying." (age fifteen)

"I wish I were shorter." (age eighteen)

"I wish I could change my nose, my thighs, my stomach, my self-esteem, and my confidence." (age fifteen)

"I wish I had the attributes of a really great friend ... understanding and patient." (age fifteen)

"I wish I could stop judging people on how they act the first time I see them." (age fifteen)

"I wish I had more self-motivation toward sports and schoolwork." (age fourteen)

"I wish I were more athletic and less lazy in school." (age seventeen)

"I wish I were more interesting and likeable." (age sixteen)

"I wish I wasn't so loud and obnoxious when I get excited about stuff." (age seventeen)

"I wish I were more artsy and not so shy." (age eighteen)

"I wish I was more physically fit." (age seventeen)

"I wish I had green eyes, not brown; that I had wavy hair, not flat; that I was 5'8", not 5'5", and that I never had any injuries so I wouldn't get behind in athletics." (age fifteen)

"I wish my hair were perfectly straight." (age fifteen)

"I wish my hands weren't so big." (age fourteen)

"I wish I didn't have acne." (age fourteen)

"I wish I would think before I act." (age fourteen)

"I wish I had some self-discipline." (age fourteen)

"I wouldn't change anything. You have to deal with what you've
     got!" (age sixteen)

Some of the wishes involve outer changes. Some, inner. I believe *each girl* (even the girl who wrote that last answer) has at least one thing she'd like to change about herself. And that's not all bad. After all, if you're a lazy person, and you know it and you want to change it — well, that's a good thing, right? Or if you're super shy, and you know it and you want to work at being at least a little more outgoing, that can be a good thing too, right?

But what if you want to be taller (high heels, I guess), or shorter (slouch, I suppose), or have green instead of blue eyes (colored contact lenses), or have smaller hands (can't think of anything)? Those things can't be changed, even with the short-term "solution." They're part of who we are. They're things we have to learn to accept and love about ourselves, or we'll waste energy and tears.

I want you to go back through the list you made and do a few things. First, decide which things *can't* be changed and which things *can* be changed. Be honest, and realistic. For example, if you're a person who wishes for a different body shape or that you weighed less, that might be a changeable thing if you have some eating habits that could be improved (cutting out junk food, for example) and if you're not a very active person (start moving around more). But if you already eat decently and are at least moderately active, then nothing you do — unless you start one of those seriously intense and insane workout programs, or unless you do something dangerous and unhealthy — is going to change your weight or body shape. *And that's okay!* So now go back and put an X by the things in your list that *can't* be changed and a check mark by the things that *can* be changed.

Now take a look at the things in your list that *can't* be changed. Try to figure out why you're so unhappy or discontent with those things. Is it because of something someone said to you? Or maybe because you're comparing yourself to some impossible cultural ideal? Whatever the reason is, here's what you need to try and figure out: *Why* do you want those things to be different? Obviously you must believe your life will be better if those things are changed ... but *why*? Being taller would mean you could see above the crowd instead of looking at everyone's chin, true. Just like being a size eight instead of a size ten would mean you could buy different sized jeans or having curly hair instead of straight hair (or the other way around) would mean you could try out different hairstyles. But how would any of those things make life better for you?

One of the first steps to surviving a Skin crisis is to accept the things that can't be changed. There's an old prayer that you've probably seen on a bookmark or greeting card, or maybe on a plaque or picture hanging on your grandma's wall. It goes like this:

God, grant me the serenity
to accept the things I cannot change;
courage to change the things I can;
and wisdom to know the difference.

When I was in junior high and high school, I worked at a Christian bookstore. We sold tons of stuff with that prayer on it. I probably read that prayer thousands of times while I worked at that store, but I never really paid much attention to it. I thought it was for old people — after all, it was always old people buying the bookmarks, plaques, paintings, and greeting cards. What did a prayer for old people have to do with me?

It's too bad I didn't pay closer attention because that prayer could have saved me a lot of heartache and pain. I wasted so much energy, time, and tears worrying about and trying to change things that couldn't be changed instead of accepting them and being content. My hope for you is that you can learn *now* to start accepting unchangeable things and to let go of things you have no control over. When you do, you'll have made a huge step toward working through your own Skin crisis.

But that's not enough. I believe God desires each of us to become the best we can be, and that means tackling the changeable things on our list in a positive way too. I'm not talking about a self-help or self-improvement program that guarantees to make you successful and popular in "three easy steps or your money back (and we'll throw in a set of professional cooking knives AND a clap-on-clap-off lightswitch AND a case of miracle stain-remover FOR FREE IF YOU ORDER NOW!!!)." I'm talking about change that's more than skin deep — change that reflects God's will and Word — change that's intentional and focused and practiced. Some things only God can change through his transforming power. But some things you can take an active role in changing (though they may very well require God's help as well). It takes courage to begin making those changes, and it'll probably take time for them to really take shape.

Just like we did before with the things that *can't* be changed, it's important to look at the reasons why you want to make the changes that *can* be made — because, quite honestly, some people have bad reasons for wanting to make good changes.

But first, here are some good reasons girls gave for the changes they want to make in their lives:

"I want to think things out before acting, because I keep embarrassing myself with that." (age fourteen)

"I wish I were more outgoing, because I don't really know how to start a conversation." (age sixteen)

"I wish I were less lazy in school, because when college comes around, studying is going to be necessary, so I'd better learn some skills and techniques now." (age seventeen)

"I wish I could change the way I judge people before I know them, because I could have so many more friends, and I would be open to new people and new things and opportunities." (age seventeen)

"I wish I could have more confidence, because I want to believe in myself and love myself." (age fifteen)

"I want to be more outgoing, because I don't want to scare away people who could become good friends or mentors by being antisocial." (age eighteen)

"I wish it was easier for me to jump right into new groups and conversations, because I want to be able to influence people and show them what they could have if God were part of their lives." (age sixteen)

"I wish I realized what I was saying and doing before I do it, because I've lost a lot of friends by not thinking before I act." (age seventeen)

"I want to change my attitude, because it gets me into trouble a lot." (age eighteen)

"I wish that I wasn't shy around people I don't know, because I want to be secure about myself." (age sixteen)

"I want to be healthier, because I want to live a long life, and I don't want to hide or feel ashamed of myself." (age sixteen)

"I wish that I were more outgoing, because I want to feel comfortable in new situations." (age thirteen)

"I want to be closer to God, because sometimes I just feel so lost." (age fourteen)

I think these are good reasons for wanting to make changes in yourself. And now for the bad reasons girls want to make (inner or outer) personal changes — or more specifically, the worst reason: "Because I'll be happier."

There are lots of beautiful people who aren't happy. There are lots of rich people who aren't happy. There are lots of tall people who aren't happy. There are lots of famous people who aren't happy. There are lots of thin people who aren't happy. There are lots of outgoing people who aren't happy. There are lots of athletic people who aren't happy. (Get it?)

"Happy" is not a good or reliable way to measure the health of your Skin. It's true that many people with Skin crises are unhappy, but "happy" actually isn't the opposite of "unhappy." (I know the dictionary says it is, but the dictionary is just about words — it's not always about truth.) If you're unhappy because of a Skin crisis, the opposite is to feel content, joyful, and peaceful. You can be all those things without necessarily being "happy." We've all been fed the lie that "happy" is the goal, and that just isn't true. Happiness depends on circumstances (which continually change) and on our immediate reactions to those circumstances (which also continually change). You could say that happiness is fleeting and shallow and only skin deep. Contentment, joy, and peace, though, are rooted deeply in what we believe and what we know to be true. They are lasting. They are more — so much more — than skin deep.

So now I want you to look at the things in your list that *can* be changed and give honest reasons why you want to change those things. Are your reasons legitimate? Would they please God? Are they related to contentment, joy, and peace? Are they more than skin deep, rooted in truth? Or are they mostly about your personal happiness?

Let's go one step further. There are probably some things you wish you could change about yourself that *can* be changed and that *should* be changed — things that have to do with unhealthy or unkind behaviors and attitudes. One of the main ways to navigate and survive your own personal Skin crisis is — after you've learned to differentiate between the can-be-changed and can't-be-changed things in life — to further differentiate between the can-be-changed-but-doesn't-have-to-be-changed and can-be-changed-and-should-be-changed things. Just because something *can* be changed doesn't mean it *needs* to be changed. So now I want you to go back to your list, look at all the things that *can* be changed, decide which are things that *should* be changed, and list them here:

Things That *Can* be Changed and *Should* be Changed:

Let's take the next step. Once you've learned to accept the things that can't be changed (a simple piece of advice that can have a huge, positive impact on your state of mind and your level of contentment) and have identified what things can (and should) be changed — which will give you a feeling of purpose and direction as you deal with your own personal Skin crisis — then the next step is to create a plan and goal for how you're going to start working on the things that should be changed.

I can't tell you how to do that because each situation is different. But at the end of this book, in "Advice from the Experts" you can read about six college-aged young women, each of whom went through her own Skin crisis. You might recognize yourself in one of their stories and learn a few things about how you can deal with your own personal Skin crisis too.

If you're not sure how to decide which things *can* be changed and which things *should* be changed, you might want to consider how each item on your list fits into God's plan for how his followers should live their lives. For example, being more outgoing is something that *can* be changed (you'll see how if you read Brooke's story later in this chapter), but is it always something that *should* be changed?

If being non-outgoing keeps you from defending yourself and friends from hurtful gossip, or if it prevents you from standing up for your faith, then it's something you should consider trying to change. But realize that if you're naturally introverted, it's unlikely that you can make yourself (and you probably shouldn't make yourself) a major extrovert. You can, though, become less introverted. You might need to say to yourself, "God made me quiet. God made my shy. And that's okay. As long as I don't let those things get in the way of living my life obediently for God, then I'm going to be a contently quiet person."

The following is one of their stories, about a young woman who saw something in her life she wanted to change — something that *could* be changed, something she thought *should* be changed, and something she *did* change by being intentional, committed, and courageous.

Brooke's Story

When Brooke was in eighth grade, she looked at a picture of herself and didn't like what she saw. "I knew what I looked like — I mean, I saw myself in the mirror every day and was just fine with it. But when I saw that particular picture, I don't know what happened. Something about it affected me so negatively. I hated the way I looked."

It was the beginning of Brooke's Skin crisis, and she remembers the moment vividly. She was also really concerned about her weight, and in her own words, became a chronic over-exerciser. "I played tennis. I ran. I did the treadmill. If I didn't exercise as much as I thought I should, or if I missed an exercise session, I would get so mad at myself."

In the end, her over-commitment to exercise caused a crisis of its own that forced her to reexamine the way she viewed herself. "I ended up ruining my knee one time when I was running really hard. That was the end of over-exercising for me. In fact, that was the end of any exercise at all for a while."

In terms of her personality, Brooke was very aware of who she was and how she acted around other people. "I was super quiet and reserved. I didn't talk much around other people. There were some other kids who were really quiet and reserved too, and one time it dawned on me that I was like that. I realized I didn't want to be that way anymore."

Several of Brooke's friends, including the queen bee of their group, were outgoing. "I decided I wanted to be more like them . . . not because I thought they were better than me or because I thought something was wrong with me, but because I realized I was missing out on some things because of my shyness."

So Brooke watched and learned. "I paid close attention to my outgoing friends — and other outgoing people I knew. I watched them carefully. I watched their reactions. I listened to the timing of their conversations. I observed it all very carefully — in a quiet, wallflowerish kind of way (I don't think anyone knew what I was doing because I was so quiet and shy about it) — and then I tried it for myself."

Brooke didn't become an outgoing, conversation-starter right away. But toward the middle of high school, she had become a leader not only of her immediate group of friends but of the whole school. "I suppose it sounds kind of unusual that I saw something I wanted to change about myself, and then I went out and did it. But it worked for me. It wasn't easy. It's probably never easy for a reserved, quiet, shy wallflower to break out of her shell. But I was determined. I knew that if I wanted to have an impact on other students and be a leader among my peers, I needed to make some changes."

Today, Brooke is a confident, strong young woman. She currently is a leader in a ministry to junior high kids, where her ability to be outgoing and confident and to welcome and mentor younger kids is key. Though Brooke has shed some of her introverted tendencies, she is still soft-spoken. After all, she has certain attributes and characteristics that God designed in her. She will probably never be the loudest or craziest person in a crowd. But she's no longer the quietest, most reserved, and shyest person, either. She identified something she wanted to change. She realized she *could* change it, and decided that she *should* change it so she could be a leader and a positive influence on those around her.

I've known Brooke for five years. She's amazing. I'm impressed with her confidence, her faith, her friendliness, and so many other things. But Brooke, like every other human being, still has things she deals with. Being in college, having survived junior and senior high, doesn't mean her life is perfect. Everyone deals with minor Skin crises throughout their lifetimes, and Brooke is no different. But those crises become less and less dramatic and traumatic the more we grow in our faith, the less we focus on ourselves, the more we focus on God, and the more comfortable we become in our own Skin.

One way to get better at those things is to pay attention to that old prayer we read before:

God, grant me the serenity to accept the things I cannot change:

(stop obsessing about things in the *can't-be-changed* list)

courage to change the things I can;

(make an action plan for the *can-be-changed-and-should-be-changed* list)

and wisdom to know the difference.

(stop stubbornly trying to turn *can't-be-changed* things into *can-be-changed* things — give it up, already!)

Going More than Skin Deep:

1. Identify at least two or three things in your can't-be-changed list that you're going to stop trying to change and start accepting. Ask one or two of your friends to help you with this, both by encouraging you and by praying for you.

2. Identify one thing in your can-be-changed-and-should-be-changed list that you're going to start working on right now. What are some immediate steps you can take to start pursuing this change? What are some long-term steps you can take?

3. Rewrite the old prayer from this chapter in your own words. Make it personal so that it fits your specific situation and Skin crisis. Start praying it daily, believing that God will give you serenity, courage, and wisdom (or whatever words you use).

chapter
4

Questions, Part I

IN CASE YOU HAVEN'T NOTICED, TODAY'S WORLD IS FULL OF ANSWERS. The Internet offers answers to every question you could possibly think of. I often type in questions like this: How can I take a color photo and remove all the colors except one? or How can I make the really delicious, chunky kind of salsa they serve in genuine Mexican restaurants? My questions are usually long and wordy and rambling, but even so, once I hit the return key — ta-da! Usually at least 1,237,413 answers show up on my screen within milliseconds.

Want to know where to buy something? Type in a question.

Want to know how to make something? Type in a question.

Want to know what a word means? Type in a question.

Want to know what will happen to your cat after she ate a whole roll of dental floss? Type in a question. (This really happened to my friend, by the way. Her cat is fine.)

When I was a kid, I had to tromp down to the library and look up my questions in a huge set of encyclopedias that were often at least twenty years old. Not anymore. Today, answers are at our fingertips. Literally.

Today's world is also full of questions, many of which are pretty superficial and skin deep. Here are some recent ones, straight from the covers of girl magazines you can find on newsstands:

Does he know you like him?

What's your summer crushin' style?

What should I wear with my boyfriend jeans?

What's your back-to-school strategy?

What are the perfect jeans for your body?

Are you secretly embarrassing?

How can I be one size smaller?

What should I wear this weekend?

What's your beach vibe?

Is it hot out here, or is it just you?

The following are titles of articles from several 1961 editions of *Seventeen*:

"Why Do I Like Music?" by Judith Olmstead, age seventeen

"What Makes Me Tick" by Hayley Mills, age fourteen, star of the original *Parent Trap*

"Are You Rosy or Tawny? Your Prettiest Colors"

"How Can I Have a Funday Sundae Party?"

"How Do I Find a Summer Job?"

The ads and articles in the 1961 issues of *Seventeen* feature fashion, shoes, complexion products, recipes, decorating tips, furniture, sewing and crafts, silverware and dishes, engagement rings (!), bras and girdles, Chef Boyardee pizza kits (the new-fangled, popular food), deodorant (a fairly new product), stockings (as in individual full-length, seamed silk stockings held in place by attaching to a girdle with these weird hooks and snaps … crazy, I know), luggage, and makeup. Wow. Times sure have changed.

What really turns him on?
How can you tell if he's a good kisser?
Is he into you?

And that's just a sampling. Many of the questions are too embarrassing or too personal to share here (which means they shouldn't be on the cover of a magazine, don't you think?). There are lots of implied questions too, such as:

How can I have perfect skin?
How can I lose ten pounds in one week?
How can I look two sizes smaller?
How can I get him to notice me?
How can I have great hair?
How can I accessorize on a tight budget?
How can I get my parents off my case?
How can I be the most popular girl in school?
How can I have more friends?
How can I have more boyfriends?
How can I be cuter?
How can I be skinnier?
How can I be taller?
How can I be awesome?
And on and on.

Almost all of these questions have one thing in common: They're about skin, and the things you wear or put on your skin. They're about the outside of you. They're exterior, and for the most part, they're shallow. Even if you found the answers to the previous questions, they wouldn't change your life or give it purpose or meaning or joy.

If you're someone who's interested in something deeper or who's experiencing a Skin crisis, the world's questions are ridiculous. They aren't going to lead you to anything of substance or importance. But there *are* some questions that are worth asking, questions that are more than skin deep, questions that aren't shallow, questions that deal with Life and Truth and Skin.

Keep reading to learn about questions that can't be answered on the Internet in the blink of an eye (or in an old set of encyclopedias on your grandmother's bookshelves) but are worth asking nonetheless. Beware: These questions deal with Skin, and they usually require some serious soul-searching on your part. And they aren't always easy or pleasant to ask yourself. After all, we're talking about Skin here. We're talking deep. It's going to take more than "What's my summer style?" to really get to the heart of the matter.

What's Wrong with Me?

I know what you're thinking: How is *that* question going to help me do anything except feel bad about myself, or worse than I already do?! Truthfully, this question *won't* help you if you ask the wrong people. According to advertisers, magazines, movies, and music, here's what's wrong with you:

- You're not tall enough.
- You're not thin enough.
- You're not pretty enough.
- Your skin isn't clear enough.
- You're not rich enough.
- You're not popular enough.
- You don't have enough friends.
- Your teeth aren't white enough.
- Your hair isn't straight/curly enough.
- Your clothes aren't stylish enough.

- Your shoes aren't funky enough.
- Your makeup isn't gorgeous enough.
- Your deodorant isn't strong enough.
- You don't have enough accessories in your closet.
- blahblahblahblahblahblah

Don't believe me? Check out the most recent magazines, ads, and infomercials. They all imply that your style/shape/size/skin/hair/teeth/odor/appearance isn't/aren't what they should be — but if you'll just buy whatever it is they're selling, then everything will be okay. You'll be happy (remember: "happy" isn't the goal anymore), and life will be grand. Advertisers are tricky people. They want you to believe that they care about you and consider you awesome, but all they really care about is your money, and what they really want is for you to feel so un-awesome that you'll plunk down your cash (or credit or debit card) to buy whatever this-or-that thing they're selling — which they know won't really make you any happier in the long run, because if it did you wouldn't buy any more of their stuff, and then they'd go out of business. What they really offer is a quick-fix-that-will-wear-off-really-soon so that you'll want to buy more of their stuff to feel good for a little while until you feel un-awesome again, which you will when you read/see/hear their ads.

Phew! Did you follow all of that?

Don't *ever* ask our culture, "What's wrong with me?" because you'll get a lot of really bad and untruthful answers.

However, this is a great question to ask God. After all, we're not talking about skin; we're talking about Skin — God's specialty — and Skin is spiritual and eternal and sacred. And even though God created you and loves you and adores you (we'll talk about that in the next chapter), God also knows there is something wrong with you, with me, with all of us. And the problem has everything to do with our Skin. With our hearts. With our very selves.

A Personal Story

I started going to church regularly from the day I was old enough to be bundled up and taken out of the house. We were a church-every-Sunday-morning-and-evening kind of family. That's just how things were. We didn't stay home for snowstorms or sickness or anything else. I don't remember much about those first few years of church. I do remember spilling communion grape juice on my mom's white gloves once (not a happy memory). I also remember being taken outside once and "being talked to" by my dad, probably because I wouldn't sit still or wouldn't be quiet during the service (also not a happy memory). I remember sitting with an old lady while my mom and dad sang in choir. I remember an old man named Art who used to give me shiny pennies. And I remember my kindergarten Sunday school teacher, a large grand-motherly woman named Mrs. Swanson.

One Sunday, Mrs. Swanson told all of us children that Jesus loved us and wanted to live in our hearts, and if we would just ask him, Jesus would live there forever. We would be God's children and would go to heaven to live with him someday. I thought that sounded good, so when Mrs. Swanson invited us, I raised my hand to say yes to Jesus, prayed a simple prayer, and I became a child of God forever.

I never doubted my faith. I never doubted that God was real. I never thought church was a scam or a joke or a total waste of time.

But when I hit junior high and high school, my faith was no longer just about a five-year-old girl raising her hand to say yes to Jesus. It was no longer just about going to church because my parents went to church. It was no longer just about Sunday-morning-and-Sunday-night attendance. Life was more complicated than that. I still knew and believed that God loved me, but my faith wasn't so simple anymore. First off, God's love meant more to me now than it had in kindergarten, because as I'd gotten older, I'd gotten to know myself better. When I was five, I wasn't surprised that God loved me. After all, who doesn't love a five-year old? But when I was a teenager, I couldn't take God's love for granted anymore because I finally was old enough to realize that there were plenty of reasons for God *not* to love me.

I wasn't very kind to my sister.

I was jealous of the beautiful girl down the street.

I looked down on some of my classmates who I was smarter than.

I didn't always tell the truth.

I downright hated some of the kids in my school.

I thought about things I shouldn't think about.

I wanted things to go my own way.

I made fun of other people in order to feel better about myself.

I didn't always respect my parents.

I often avoided opportunities to do the good and right thing.

I realized, in fact, that I was a Sinner.

At age five I knew I was a sinner. Who didn't at that age? Sometimes I was mean. Sometimes I sassed. Sometimes I pinched people I didn't like. I sinned.

But as a teenager I was mature enough to know the implications of the fact that I sinned. In fact, I was a Sinner (the capital *S* kind). In other words, my heart was desperately wicked. I wanted to live my own way, not God's. I cared about myself more than others. Yes, I sinned. But worse, I was a Sinner.

The difference between sin and Sin is sort of like the difference between skin and Skin. One is on the surface, visible, and measurable. The other is deep inside, at the core of someone's being. But sin and Sin are much more closely related than skin and Skin. All people sin because they are Sinners, so the two are inseparable, unlike skin and Skin. But while most people will admit that they sin (that there's a surface problem), not everyone will admit they are Sinners (that there's a deeper problem, a problem that only God can take care of).

A Skin crisis can be caused by a lot of things: Dissatisfaction with skin; dissatisfaction with Skin; family upheaval; friend problems; unforeseen circumstances; and Sin. That's right. Just at the age when you're dealing with a body that's going through significant changes and a brain that's working overtime, you've matured spiritually enough to recognize that there are quite possibly things in your heart that aren't right with God, that you're a Sinner, that you have a Skin issue that's spiritual as well as emotional or relational.

I don't know about your relationship with Jesus. Maybe you're like me, and you've been loving Jesus and believing in him since you were little. Or maybe you've just recently come to know Jesus and follow him. Either way, there's a good chance that your personal Skin crisis has a spiritual component to it. Regardless of how long you've known God, because of your age and maturity right now, you're probably just beginning to realize the depth of Jesus' love for you and the cost of his salvation. It's not just that he loves you ... it's that he loves you *while you were still a Sinner, while you were unlovable, while you were unworthy of his love.* That's a love that the world knows nothing about. Part of your Skin crisis might include the realization of your Sinfulness. It's true that followers of Jesus have been given a new heart — a new Skin, if you will. (See 2 Corinthians 5:17.) But it's also true that our old Skin sometimes rears up its stubborn, self-centered head and causes us to behave and speak and live in ways that aren't at all what God desires for us.

This next question I want you to think about is going to be harder than the previous ones. It's more serious. It's more important. It's more real. I want you to list things about your actions, thoughts, and words that aren't godly — things you know are either disobedient or dishonoring to God, things you know don't please God, things that aren't reflective of the new Skin you were given when you decided to follow Christ. (By the way, don't fall into the trap of listing only the bad things you do. You should also list the good things you know you should do, but don't do. If there's a kid who eats alone in your cafeteria every day, and you've thought, *I should say hi or maybe sit with her,* but never have, well, that should go on the list.)

One more thing before you start: I'm not asking you to make this list because I want you to feel badly about yourself, or because I want you to feel guilty, or because I think it's a good idea to focus on the negative things in life; I want you to make this list so you can look at it, learn from it, identify areas of your life that you haven't given totally to God — and then be amazed at God's love and forgiveness.

What words, actions, thoughts, or parts of my Skin are dishonoring or disobedient to God?

There are a few things I want you to do with this list. First, I want you to spend time confessing these things to God and asking for forgiveness. The Bible is *very clear* that if you confess your sins, God promises to forgive them (see I John 1:9). Next I want you to figure out which of these things are habits for you. In other words, maybe you've struggled with some things on your list just every now and then, but maybe other things are regular issues for you — such as gossip, lying, control, bitterness, anger, or whatever. Those are things you need to identify, admit, and give to God, asking for his power and grace to transform you.

I know a young woman who was a serious gossip when she was in high school. She was a Christian, but she didn't really feel badly or worry about being a gossip because she observed that everyone else — even her Christian friends — seemed to gossip too (which was quite possibly true, but isn't an excuse). One day something her small-group leader said convinced her about the sinfulness of her behavior. At first, she was surprised. After all, she'd gossiped for a long time and never felt badly about it, so why was she all of a sudden feeling guilty? After the surprise wore off, she started feeling badly about herself. Not just badly about the gossip, but badly about herself. "How could I be so mean? How could I have been so blind to what I was doing? It's like I just ignored God and the Bible. I'm a terrible Christian! I can't believe I was so stupid and so thoughtless and so *bad*! I'm *horrible*!"

This young woman fell into a Skin crisis that had nothing to do with her appearance or being shy or being unpopular. Hers was a spiritual Skin crisis, and it led her down a dangerous path of unnecessary guilt and fear.

Here's the deal: Her gossip *was* wrong. It *was* a sin. It *did* displease God. *But* — and this is very important — it didn't make God stop loving her. It didn't make Jesus turn his back on her. It didn't make her any less of a Christian. It did, though, strain her relationship with God. (Anytime we disobey God it puts a strain on the relationship, but it doesn't end or stop the relationship.) A spiritual Skin crisis can be a good thing *if* you respond to it correctly — by admitting the problem, asking God for forgiveness, and then surrendering yourself to God so he can work to transform your attitude and heart and Skin. But a spiritual Skin crisis can be a bad thing if you doubt God's love, your worth and value as a human being, and your salvation.

I'm not going to talk about Satan much in this book, but I'll say this — Satan loves to take a typical, normal, average Skin crisis (whether it's about appearance or personality or spiritual things) and blow it into a huge, paralyzing, crippling, debilitating, and depressing crisis that swallows you up and threatens to never let you go. Nothing makes the devil happier than you saying, "I'm so bad that God would never love me. I might as well give up on God right now because I'm sure he's given up on me." Of course, Satan's also happy when we say, "I'm so awesome that I don't care if God loves me. I love myself so much that I don't need God's love." (That's not what most people say when they're in the middle of a Skin crisis, but you get the idea.)

I've known lots of girls who've done things they were so ashamed of that they were convinced God could never love them. They had spiritual Skin crises that, if dealt with in a positive way, could have led them to God, but instead they were poisoned with fear, preventing them from ever knowing God's grace and love and kindness and gentleness and forgiveness.

Know this: God isn't pleased with our sins. He expects us to sin less and less as we become and more and more like Jesus. Paul's letter to the Colossians (a short book in the New Testament that you should read tonight) talks about this a lot. It tells us to stand firm in the truth, to not drift away from what we know is right, to keep following Jesus closely, and to set aside — "put to death" is the actual phrase — our sinful attitudes and habits. Yes, God forgives us when we confess, but that's not something we should take advantage of. It always amazes me when I hear someone say, "I know I shouldn't do this, but God will forgive me." I don't think that's the way it's supposed to work, do you? At the same time, we're not God, we're not perfect, and we're not sinless. We will always struggle to live like Jesus did, and it will always be a challenge to become more and more like him. *But that's still the goal!* Philippians 2:5 says we should have the same mindset as Jesus. Our mindset, or attitude, is the thing that drives our words and actions, so as it becomes more and more like Jesus', there will be less and less sin in our lives.

The answer to the question, "What's wrong with me?" is this: We are fallen, Sinful humans who can't do enough good things to be good enough for God. We are self-centered, selfish people who want things our own way. We are petty, childish mortals who would like to be our own gods instead of letting God be our one and only God. We are hurtful, spiteful beings who usually think more of ourselves than we think of others. And all of that leads to spiritual death.

That pretty much sums it up. So much for trying to survive a Skin crisis, eh? If you stop reading right now, you might spiral down into the deepest Skin crisis of your life — which is why you shouldn't stop reading. The next question will help you turn a corner and head in a direction that will change your life, not just today, but forever.

Going More than Skin Deep:

1. Why do you think we so easily brush off some sins as unimportant but view others as so bad that God won't forgive them?
2. Think about how much of your Skin crisis is due to spiritual things. Why do you suppose our spiritual health and emotional health are so closely related?
3. Read Colossians 3:1 – 10. Are there any issues in these verses that you struggle with? What will you do, starting right now, to begin eliminating those things from your life?

chapter
5

Questions, Part II

"Every young girl wants to understand herself. And why not? She must live with herself the rest of her days." (from *Strictly Confidential,* 1944)

WHEN I WAS IN THE FIFTH GRADE, MY MOM TOOK ONE OF MY RED T-shirts and used iron-on letters to put my name on the front. "Crystal" didn't fit, so she shortened it to "Crys," which is what a lot of my friends and family called me anyway.

I was pretty excited the first day I wore that shirt to school. That probably sounds silly to you, but this was in the days before most T-shirts had anything printed on them. To get a printed or personalized T-shirt, you had to make it yourself. Anyway, I walked into school, and one of my friends saw the shirt and said, "Cool! Where'd you get it?" I proudly told her my mom made it. I could tell it was going to be a good day.

Then I walked into my classroom, and a boy named Danny looked at my shirt, looked at me, and said, "Cries? Cries? Why does your shirt say 'cries'?" (Ha ha. Danny, the class clown, was pronouncing "crys" phonetically, which was *sooooooo* clever of him.) I said, "It says 'Crys,' stupid, which is my name, as everyone with half a brain knows." He laughed. "Well, joke's on you, cuz your shirt says your name is 'cries,' which is hysterical. Cries! Cries! Ha!!! That's perfect cuz girls always cry anyway. Cries! Cries! Hey, everyone, come look at Cries' shirt!"

I wanted to kick him, which I knew I shouldn't (even though I'd kicked him once in third grade after he'd pelted me with a kickball during recess). I wanted to hit him, which I also knew I shouldn't. I wanted to call him something mean, which, yes, I knew once again I shouldn't (and I couldn't think of anything, anyway). All my joy about my new T-shirt — which seems pretty silly now — was ruined because that kid kept calling me the wrong name and was laughing at me about it. "Cries." Wow. How stupid could he be?

Who Am I?

It's the most basic question we can ask ourselves. And we can ask it in different ways: It can be asked in a genuine spirit of wonder — Who *am* I? Or it can be asked with a sarcastic spirit of bitterness — Who am *I*? The words are the same, but the implications of each question are vastly different.

Think of it another way: Let's say you get invited to a party or concert or retreat or whatever event would excite you. You don't know many people who are going. You don't even know the person who invited you. You're there because a friend of a friend told someone to include you. So far, so good. You arrive, walk in, see a crowd of people you don't know, and then someone you assume is the hostess approaches you. She walks over, smiles, and says, "Hi! Who are you?" in a friendly, inviting voice. (You'll have to provide the tone and inflection yourself to hear what I'm talking about. Just say the words quickly and make your voice rise higher with each word.) You smile back and tell her your name. She says, "I'm so glad you came!" It's all good. You start to breathe easy again, confident you're going to have a great time.

Now imagine it happens this way: You arrive, walk in, see a crowd of people you don't know, and then someone you assume is the hostess approaches you. She walks over, studies you for a few seconds, raises an eyebrow, purses her lips together, and says, "Who are you?" in a snobbish, snotty, condescending tone. (You'll have to provide the tone and inflection yourself to hear what I'm talking about. Just say "who" firmly and slowly, then say "are" more quietly and quickly, and then say "you" firmly and slowly. Can you hear the icky tone?) You mutter something about being a friend of so-and-so and getting an invitation and thinking it would be okay to show up and apologizing if there's a problem. And she says, "Um, *yeah*, there *is* a problem!" at which point you turn around and walk away before anyone sees how miserable and embarrassed you are.

The same question — Who are you? — can have totally different meanings.

One can mean, "I'm so glad you're here and I'd like to get to know you," and the other can mean, "You have no right to be here, let alone exist at all, and I never want to see you again."

It's the same way with the question "Who am I?" It can have totally different meanings, depending on how you ask it. If you ask yourself that question in an inviting, kind, friendly way it means you really want to get to know yourself, that you're really interested in who you are, that you really care about your Skin. But if you ask yourself that question in a condescending, bitter, unhappy, angry, sarcastic way, it means you've already decided that you don't like yourself, that you wish you were someone else, and that you don't like your Skin at all.

I believe too many people ask "Who am I?" the second way, which is a shame. Since God created you, it's absolutely worth taking the time to get to know yourself and figure out the answer to that question.

The most obvious answer is your name. "I am Katelyn." "I am Jessica." "I am Rachel." "I am Crystal." (I am *not* "Cries," okay?) Your name is a significant part of your identity. If you've ever had an unwelcome nickname (such as "Stucky"), or if anyone has ever continually called you by the wrong name, you know what I'm talking about. Little kids know this inherently. They quickly correct people who call them by the wrong names. "I'm not Caitlin. I'm Katie!" When my youngest son started school, he no longer wanted to be called T.J., short for Tate Jacob. He wanted to be called Tate. It was very important to him that his teachers, his friends, and his family use the name he wanted. It was part of his identity, part of his self, part of his Skin.

But there's so much more to "Who am I?" than just your name.

After spending the first few years of my life in a small Nebraska farming community, my family moved to the Chicago suburbs. I was born on the prairie, but I was raised in the land of strip malls, super-highways, tollbooths, asphalt, and one of the world's busiest airports . . . much to my chagrin. There was nothing exciting about being a suburbanite. It was boring. It was passé. It was deathly dull. I wanted to be different from everyone else. Special. Unique. And so I always made sure my friends knew that my grandfather was a cowboy. I would proudly show them pictures of him wearing his cowboy boots and his cowboy hat, astride a large horse, looking proud and strong and manly and definitely non-suburbanish. Being his granddaughter was a big part of my "Who am I?" answer.

My other grandparents were from Norway. They came to America by boat, worked hard to carve out a life for themselves, and spoke Norwegian around the house, which was almost as cool as being a cowboy. They were part of my "Who am I?" answer too. For a while, my dad owned his own business where I sometimes worked. The business was part of my "Who am I?" answer. My mom could sew all kinds of amazing things, and for every holiday and other special events, my sister and I wore gorgeous dresses that our mom made by hand. Her creativity and skill were part of my "Who am I?" answer as well. My list could go on and on and on.

Our families help shape us. They're a big part of the fabric and texture of our lives. They are part of our Skin. In today's world, which more often than not makes fun of families in television shows and movies, it's easy to forget that our family's contribution to our "Who am I?" answer can be a really good thing.

Of course, it can also be a not-so-good thing.

That's the case for my friend Anna. She never knew her mom, who left when Anna was still really little. Anna's dad has been in and out of prison for as long as she can remember. In many ways, Anna has had to be the parent in the family. Her dad is part of her "Who am I?" answer. She's learned a lot from the decisions and mistakes he's made. She still loves him. She still cares about him. But she doesn't want to be like him. A few years ago, Anna was placed with an amazing foster family. They, too, are part of Anna's "Who am I?" answer.

Your name, your parents, your grandparents, your place of birth, where you grew up, your heritage — these are all part of your "Who am I?" answer. Your appearance, even though it's only skin deep, is also part of your "Who am I?" answer. Just look at your school ID or driver's license. There's a picture of you, and sometimes even information such as your height, weight, and eye and hair color. Even though that data is only skin deep, it's also part of your "Who am I?" answer.

I am a short, pale, blonde, blue-eyed, round-faced, Scandinavian-American. It's part of my identity. It's part of who I am. Even though it's just the exterior part of me, it's still part of me. But it's not the defining or most important part of me.

For that, I need to get to know my Skin.

To do that you have to answer "Who am I?" kind of like this: "I am someone who — *even though I'm not worthy, and even though I fall far short of his perfection* (remember the last chapter?) — is deeply, desperately, sincerely, ridiculously, seriously, and eternally loved by God, the creator of the universe! Not only am I loved by God, but I am created by God. I am God's masterpiece — and being short, pale, and round-faced isn't an accident. It's a design. A sacred and holy design."

You might have heard part of Psalm 139 before, but I want you to read it again. Read it carefully. Pay attention to what it says. This psalm was written by David, a guy who had more than his fair share of Skin crises. (Seriously, he was forever going through difficult situations, asking God why his life was so hard, why he was so unhappy, why things couldn't be better, why he wasn't someone different, why everyone picked on him, and why his problems were so huge.)

> For you created my inmost being;
> you knit me together in my mother's womb.
> I praise you because I am fearfully and wonderfully made;
> your works are wonderful,
> I know that full well.
> My frame was not hidden from you
> when I was made in the secret place, when I was woven together in
> the depths of the earth.
> Your eyes saw my unformed body; all the days ordained for me were
> written in your book before one of them came to be.
> How precious to me are your thoughts,[a] God!
> How vast is the sum of them!
> Were I to count them, they would outnumber the grains of sands.
>
> *Psalm 139:13 – 18a*

Here's how those verses read in different Bible translations:

> You made all the delicate, inner parts of my body
> and knit me together in my mother's womb.
> Thank you for making me so wonderfully complex!

Your workmanship is marvelous — how well I know it.
You watched me as I was being formed in utter seclusion,
as I was woven together in the dark of the womb.
You saw me before I was born.
Every day of my life was recorded in your book.
Every moment was laid out
before a single day had passed.
How precious are your thoughts about me, O God.
They cannot be numbered!
I can't even count them;
they outnumber the grains of sand!

Psalm 139:13 – 18a, NLT

Oh yes, you shaped me first inside, then out;
you formed me in my mother's womb.
I thank you, High God — you're breathtaking!
Body and soul, I am marvelously made!
I worship in adoration — what a creation!
You know me inside and out,
you know every bone in my body;
You know exactly how I was made, bit by bit,
how I was sculpted from nothing into something.
Like an open book, you watched me grow from conception to birth;
all the stages of my life were spread out before you,
The days of my life all prepared
before I'd even lived one day.

Psalm 139:13 – 16, The Message

Wow!!

You were designed, planned, and shaped *by God*. God took *nothing* and turned it into *you*. God *sculpted* you. God *formed* you. God *knit* you. God *created* **you**.

Quite honestly, that should take your breath away. The same God who made the oceans ... the same God who made the mountains ...

the same God who made the stars and the galaxies ... the same God who made the sun and the moon and the planets ... the same God who made the wind and the air and the skies ... the same God who made all of that also made ... *you*.

But instead of being amazed by that, we too often look in the mirror and think, God, couldn't you have made me a little taller? A little smaller? Couldn't you have given me a straighter nose? Bigger eyes? Nicer smile? Couldn't you have given me a great singing voice? An artist's touch? A poet's words? Couldn't you have made me, well, *better* than you did?!?!

It sounds kind of ridiculous when you consider the truth of David's psalm, doesn't it? And yet we all ask those questions to some degree rather than being amazed at what God created. Think about it: This God—who can take our breath away with his majesty, power, strength, goodness, creativity, and love—looks at you ... *you* ... and says, "You— yes, *you*—my own child, my own creation, my own design ... *YOU take my breath away!*"

Can you even begin to imagine what that means? The God of the universe, the God of *everything*, looks at each of us and is so moved by how much he loves us that he's the one left breathless. It seems pretty childish and petty and thankless to respond with, "Well, God, I know you think I'm pretty awesome and all, and I know you made me and everything, and I know you really love me, and I know you designed me and whatnot, but, um, well, do you think you might possibly con- sider making a few last-minute adjustments to the blueprint? I mean, seriously, you can't possibly expect me to live like this, can you? Have you seen the size of these feet you gave me?! Get real! Do you *know* what today's shoe styles are like?! I mean, you know everything, right? So surely you could have had enough brains (sorry, I don't mean to be rude or disrespectful, but seriously ...) to make my feet smaller! And this hair. Give me a break. It's positively impossible to do *anything* with this hair! And while we're at it, what's with all the freckles and zits? You know what … maybe you should have consulted a Perfect Girl manual before you started on me because, let's face it, you totally messed up!"

You've probably never said it quite that way before, but I bet a lot of you have thought something kind of like this. Like we said at the beginning, it's hard to be a girl in today's culture. There's a lot of pressure to look a certain way. There's an unrealistic standard of beauty.

On top of that we live in a fallen and sinful world that isn't the way God wanted it, so sometimes things happen that quite possibly weren't part of God's original, perfect plan. I don't know if God originally intended everyone to have straight teeth and perfect eyesight and clear skin. All I know is that in this world, people have all kinds of teeth, eyesight, noses, shapes, sizes, and skin … and God loves each and every one of them.

My first niece, Alisa, was a healthy, full-term baby, but shortly after she was born, the doctors diagnosed her with Down syndrome. I don't have answers to why that happened. Did God *want* her to have Down syndrome? Did God *plan* it that way? Did God form her so that her ears were small, her eyelids were tiny, her thumbs were stiff, and her heart had a malfunction? Or did something go wrong while she was being formed in her mother's womb, something that God didn't plan, but something that God allowed because this is a fallen, imperfect world? I don't know. What I do know is this: When God looked at Alisa, both while she was being formed and after she was born, God adored her, was amazed by her, and loved her so much that she *took God's breath away*. The questions of "why did God allow it?" or "why didn't God prevent it?" or "did God plan it that way?" are questions that none of us can answer in this lifetime and that won't matter when we get to heaven, because there we'll all have new bodies that will be "perfect," whatever that means in heaven.

For now, however, we are who we are, just as we are, with all our limitations — but also with all our talents, skills, abilities, and passions.

Those are the things we'll talk about now, because one of the best things you can do for yourself when you're having a Skin crisis is to get to know yourself better.

Now, that may sound strange. You might be thinking, I already know myself really well and that's exactly *why* I'm having a Skin crisis ... because I don't like myself! But I would respond with: The real problem isn't that you don't like yourself but that you don't know yourself very well. You may be skeptical about this, but just go with it for a while, okay?

Where Do You Fit?

A few years ago I read a book for teenagers called *Find Your Fit: Dare to Act on God's Design for You* by Jane Kise and Kevin Johnson. The subtitle is "How Your Talents, Spiritual Gifts, and Personality Add Up to You!"And I couldn't have read it at a better time. Even though I was an adult, far beyond the teen years, I was having a fairly serious Skin crisis. I thought it was because of my circumstances and because of my own shortcomings, but it turns out it was mostly due to me not knowing myself very well. Because I didn't really know what made me tick, I'd pursued some jobs and friendships and other things that didn't fit very well with who God had made me to be, and consequently I was miserable. If that book had been around when I was in high school and college, I really think my major teen Skin crisis would have been less painful and wouldn't have lasted as long as it did. I highly recommend that you pick up a copy of *Find Your Fit* and read it. Better yet, read it with a friend or two so you can talk about it and encourage each other.

In the meantime, here are some things you can do to start getting to know yourself better. I've done these activities with lots and lots of girls. They're not going to turn your life around suddenly. They're not going to make you the center of attention at school tomorrow. They're not going to guarantee that you make the varsity team or the top cheering squad

In junior high my friend Miriam and I decided we wanted to be Olympic athletes. Runners, to be specific. We decided we would run each day, slowly increasing our distance, until we were good enough to be on the Olympic team. Why? Because we wanted to do something that would make us important and famous and well-known. The fact that we chose running is hysterical for several reasons. First, neither Miriam nor I were athletically talented. I mean, seriously ... we couldn't win a sprint in gym class if our lives depended on it, but we were naive enough to believe we could be Olympic runners. I'm not saying it's bad to pursue a dream. But if that dream has nothing to do with who you really are or if it doesn't fit your personality or your abilities, well, there are better ways to spend your time. Second, neither Miriam nor I knew anything about running. We just liked the idea of being fast and famous runners. Third, neither Miriam nor I had any idea what we were doing. "Let's just run a little more each day until we're good enough to be in the Olympics" is one of the most ridiculous and far-fetched things I've ever heard. How about, "Let's run a little more each day until we *discover* if we even like to run, and until we *discover* if we're good enough to maybe, possibly, make the school track team, and then let's take it from there." What's even funnier is that I actually *hate* running. It makes me tired and sweaty and short of breath. It makes my sides hurt. It makes my shins hurt. It makes my head hurt. It makes me cranky. Fourth, neither Miriam nor I were really committed to running. We were just committed to the idea of being great at something—and hey, why not running? Anyway, you get the idea. It wasn't *bad* that Miriam and I had this plan (which, by the way, lasted about four days). In fact, I believe that trying out a lot of different activities and interests is a good thing. But if we know ourselves well, we'll pour our energies into trying activities and interests that have a better chance of fitting who we are.

or first chair in band. But they will help you start answering the question "Who am I?" and that's a much better question to answer than, "Does this bathing suit make me look fat?" (That's *such* a stupid and typical question in our culture, isn't it? How about, "Is this bathing suit modest enough so that I won't embarrass myself and other people at the beach?" Or how about, "Is this bathing suit suitable for public viewing?" Or maybe, "Is this bathing suit good for, oh, swimming and diving and playing in the water, which is the point of wearing a bathing suit in the first place?" The bathing suit issue will come up again later — can you tell how much it irritates me?)

Step One: Describe in writing your outer appearance — impartially

That's right. List your height, hair color, eye color, and skin color. List any other details you want — impartially, remember. No commentary allowed. Just the facts. This is who you are on the outside. It doesn't define your value or worth. But it's part of you. There's no reason to be embarrassed or upset or anything else. Write it down. Own it. Be content. Remind yourself that when God looks at you, God adores you and you take his breath away. You need to believe that. If you don't believe that (it's right there in Psalm 139), then why should you believe anything else in the Bible? This step isn't necessarily going to help you know yourself better, but it'll help you get beyond outer appearances — beyond skin. By acknowledging your skin, by describing it, by listing it, you can get it out of the way so you can move onto other things, deeper things — Skin things.

My Appearance

Step Two: Draw a picture (stick figures are fine) of the people you live with

This will probably be your immediate family, but for some people it might be different. Include whoever lives in your house. These people are part of who you are. They're part of your identity. They have a defining effect on you. Now think about your relationship with each person: Is it encouraging? Is it joyful? Is it friendly and helpful? Are there things you can do to improve the relationship? Are there things you and that person need to discuss and work on? What does it mean to be someone's daughter? Someone's sister? Someone's niece or granddaughter? How do those relationships and roles define you?

People I Live With

Step Three: Make a list of things you're good at

If your first thought is, *I'm not good at anything*, then you need to stop for a minute, take a deep breath, and remind yourself that *God designed and planned and created me. Therefore, I'm definitely good at something!* Too often we pay attention only to certain kinds of talents or abilities — usually the up-front, public, outward, fame-inducing ones. Nothing wrong with those qualities, if you have them. But for this list, you need to think outside the box too. You need to think more than skin deep. Don't just list things that fall into the athletic or artistic categories. If you're good with little kids, list that. If you can make people laugh by helping them see the good side of things, list that. If you can sense when people are having a bad day and then you go out of your way to listen to them or encourage them, list that. If you're a good organizer, list that. If you understand difficult things in your classes, things that other people just don't get, list that. List *any* and *every* skill and ability you have.

Things I'm Good At

Step Four: Make a list of all the things you're passionate about

Music. Art. Volleyball. Friendships. Books. Nature. God. Family. Dark chocolate. Chicago Bears football. Whatever. If most of the things on your list have to do with skin-deep things — such as clothes and phones and texting — then think harder. Think deeper. There are other things that matter to you, too, things that are Skin deep.

Things I'm Passionate About

Now make a list of your Top Fives in the following categories:

Books:

1.

2.

3.

4.

5.

Movies:

1.

2.

3.

4.

5.

Bands/Musicians:

1.

2.

3.

4.

5.

Songs:

1.

2.

3.

4.

5.

Games:

1.

2.

3.

4.

5.

Things to do with my friends:

1.

2.

3.

4.

5.

Places to go:

1.

2.

3.

4.

5.

Family memories:

1.

2.

3.

4.

5.

Favorite teachers:

1.

2.

3.

4.

5.

Look at your Top Five lists and ask yourself *why* these are your Top Five. What do these lists say about your interests, your passions, and your Skin?

Step Five: Make a list of things you believe and know about God and Jesus

Don't just regurgitate prayers or creeds you've learned at church — though you can start with those if you want. And don't just list things you *think* or have been *taught*. Think about what *you* believe and know about God and Jesus, and list those. These things should be the foundation for your life—for your actions, words, thoughts, and decisions. If this list isn't very long, or if you discover that you don't really believe many things about God and Jesus, then it's time to pull out your Bible and start reading. I would suggest starting with the Psalms, then moving on to the gospel of Mark (for a quick read about Jesus) and then the shorter letters of Paul (Galatians, Ephesians, Philippians, Colossians). And it's time to get plugged into a youth group or a Bible study or other group where you can start talking and learning about these things.

Things I Believe about God and Jesus

Step Six: Describe what you want your life to look like in one, five, and ten years

You can be as general or as detailed as you want. I don't want this to be a pressure thing—you get enough of that from adults trying to get you to decide *now* what degree or career you want to pursue for the rest of your life. Relax. Take a deep breath. Slow down! If you know what kind of job or career you want, fine. Include that. But if you don't, that's totally okay. This answer is less about specific job and career than it is about who you are as a person, your Skin.

For "one year," you might include things like:

- taking an art class for the first time, just to see if I like it
- making decisions about college — Do I want to go? Why? Where? When?
- being a better listener for my friends
- finding a place where I can serve others in the community

For "five years," you might include things like:

- attending college, studying for a job where I can work with people
- doing summer mission or camp work

For "ten years," well, the sky's the limit.

What I Want My Life to Look Like after One Year

What I Want My Life to Look Like after Five Years

What I Want My Life to Look Like after Ten Years

Step Seven: Describe the steps you take when faced with a decision

In some situations you need to decide between an obviously good choice (which you might really *not* want to do) and an obviously bad choice (which you might really *want* to do). How do you weigh the consequences of the two options so that you can finally decide one way or the other?

In other situations you need to make decisions between two things that are equally good. This can be just as hard, or harder, than deciding between a good and a bad thing. In these situations, most people would really like it if God would just tell us which choice to make. But more often than not, God doesn't roll like that. What then? Who do you talk to? How do you compare your choices?

Identifying how you make decisions will help you know yourself better. If you don't have a plan for decision-making, this is a good time to come up with one. It should include a spiritual element (prayer), an intellectual element (comparing the pros and cons, doing some information gathering, learning more about the options), and a relational element (talking to people you trust, asking for advice, seeking counsel). You have a lifetime of choices ahead of you. You need to have a plan for how you'll approach them.

How I Make Decisions

Step Eight: Describe your personality

This is pretty open-ended, but what I want you to do is think about where you are on a continuum of opposite personality traits. Here's a few to get you started:

introverted and shy _____ extroverted and outgoing

quiet _____ loud

funny_____ serious

leader _____ follower

people person _____ loner

emotional _____ rational

short-tempered_____ patient

(Add some of your own opposites and then place yourself on the lines.)

There are lots of personality tests you can take. Some of the online and magazine ones are quick and rather superficial. Others, like the one in *Find Your Fit*, are more detailed and in-depth, with great explanations for what your results mean. The listed pairs of opposites are just a starting point for you to think about your unique personality.

If you have distinct personality traits that don't fit on a continuum of opposites, that's okay. List those too.

Step Nine: Describe someone you admire

You can describe more than one person. At least one of them should be an adult — someone who's had a lot of life experience, has gone through some of their own Skin crises, and exhibits characteristics that you admire and want to emulate. Then ask yourself *why* you admire this person. The answers to that question will help you know yourself by showing what characteristics and personality traits you admire.

People I Admire and Reasons I Admire Them

Step Ten: Ask several people — family, friends, youth pastor, mentor, etc. — to help you get to know yourself better

Ask them to be honest. Tell them you want to know both the good and the not-so-good. Ask them to tell you what they believe your talents and abilities are, what they believe your strengths are, what they believe you could work on improving, and what they believe your personality traits are. Be sure to ask people you trust and who've known you for a while. The following are some questions you could ask them to answer (either via email, an old-fashioned letter, or a face-to-face conversation):

How would you describe my personality?
What do you believe my natural talents and abilities are?
What gifts do you believe God has given me?
What are some good things you see in my personality or attitude?
What things can I improve in my personality or my attitude?

Bonus Step (anything after ten is a bonus, isn't it?)

Describe a time or times when you felt the most confident, most yourself, and most comfortable in your own Skin. Then describe a time or times when you felt the most unconfident, most unsure of yourself, and most uncomfortable in your own Skin. These moments aren't necessarily reflections of what you'll do with the rest of your life — in other words, something that makes you uncomfortable now may be something you learn to do easily over the course of your life — but thinking about these things will still help you get to know yourself better.

That was a lot of thinking and writing. But, hey, it's important to get to know yourself. (Just for the record, I believe it's even more important that you get to know God, which is best done by spending time reading your Bible and joining a Bible study or small group.) The answer to "Who am I?" is crucial to getting through a Skin crisis. "What's my summer style?" and "How can I get him to notice me?" and "Is your best friend *really* your best friend?" aren't going to help you with a Skin crisis. In some cases, they're just going to make things worse. But getting to know you — a God-designed, God-planned, God-created, God-adored, one-of-a-kind-you — is crucial.

I'm not suggesting that you're the most important person in the universe, or that the world revolves around you, or that you should spend all your time thinking about and focusing on yourself. That, too, will lead to a Skin crisis of monumental proportions. I'm merely suggesting that since you are going to spend the rest of your life with you, and since you are valuable and beloved in God's eyes, and since God has a purpose for your life, taking some time to get to know you is time well spent.

Going More than Skin Deep:

1. What's one new thing you learned about yourself after going through the ten steps?
2. How will knowing that new thing change how you think about yourself?
3. You take God's breath away ... How does that make you feel?

PAUSE:

Now that we've talked about skin versus Skin, the Skin crisis, and some questions worth asking and answering, it's time to look at some practical and specific ways you can start living a full, joyful, and meaningful life, *even if you're in the middle of a Skin crisis.*

Some of you probably hoped this book would tell you how to end a Skin crisis or how to fix it. But honestly, a Skin crisis is one of those things that can't be solved, fixed, or eliminated. Usually it's something that needs to be lived through, dealt with, and navigated.

Jesus never promised that our lives would be crisis-free. He never promised that life would be easy. He never promised that life would be smooth sailing. In fact, just the opposite is true. He said that in this life you'll have troubles, problems, challenges, heartaches, and despair. Some are going to be more superficial (one girl I know is having a crisis because she can't choose between two good colleges) and some are going to be even deeper than Skin deep (one girl who helped with this book is, at this very minute as I write these words, by her mom's bedside at the hospital, watching her die from cancer).

That's the way life is. But if you're a Jesus follower, you don't have to go through troubles, problems, challenges, heartaches, and despair — and a Skin crisis — alone. Jesus is right there with you, walking alongside you, holding your hand tightly, even if it doesn't seem like it.

So the next few chapters are going to give you some ideas about how to step out boldly and courageously, even if you feel wallflowerish and afraid. We're going to look at our culture's top four "answers" to a skin crisis — beauty, fashion, shoes, and boyfriends — and turn them upside-down to reveal some genuine ways to deal with a Skin crisis. Beauty, fashion, shoes, and boyfriends (or romance) are the most advertised, most photographed, most talked-about, and most written-about things in popular magazines and television ads and other kinds of media. The message is, "If you are only beautiful enough, wear the right fashions, own enough shoes, and have an awesome boyfriend, then YOU WILL BE HAPPY AND LIFE WILL BE PERFECT!"

To which I say — bah. Feh. Baloney. Pshaw. Nonsense. Hokum. Bunkum. Rubbish. Pish posh. Hoo hah snit snot. No way.

Read on to find out why.

chapter
6

Beauty

"The age of beauty will never come until every woman takes a bath every day." (from *Personal Beauty*, 1870)

"When a girl paints and powders till she looks like an advertisement for cosmetics, she shows a foolish heart, which is not beautiful." (from *Beautiful Girlhood*, 1922)

"Without true beauty of soul a pretty face is a dangerous gift." (from *Beautiful Girlhood*, 1922)

Charm is deceptive, and beauty is fleeting; but a woman who fears the LORD is to be praised.
— Proverbs 31:30

Your beauty should not come from outward adornment, such as elaborate hairstyles and the wearing of gold jewelry or fine clothes. Rather, it should be that of your inner self, the unfading beauty of a gentle and quiet spirit, which is of great worth in God's sight. — 1 Peter 3:3–4

"Woe to you, teachers of the law and Pharisees, you hypocrites! You are like whitewashed tombs, which look beautiful on the outside but on the inside are full of the bones of the dead and everything un-clean." — Matthew 23:27

ONE OF THE MOST BEAUTIFUL WOMEN I'VE EVER KNOWN WAS NOT very beautiful by the world's standards. Her name was Miss Rau, and she taught fifth-grade Sunday school at my church. Miss Rau was old. I don't know how old, just old. She was short, as in under-five-feet-tall short. She slouched, which made her even shorter. She had short brown hair that had absolutely no particular style at all. She wore brown old-lady shoes, orthopedic stockings (and sometimes anklets on top of those), and shapeless housedresses. She had tiny, old-fashioned glasses, and when she got cataracts, her eyes were pink and watery and runny. She didn't wear makeup. She didn't wear jewelry. She didn't use perfume. She didn't have high cheekbones, a shapely chest-waist-hip ratio, porcelain skin, or entrancing eyes. She didn't have luxurious hair, or elegant hands, or fabulous bone structure. She didn't smell like roses, walk with a sophisticated stride, or have a voice like an angel.

She was old. She was small. She was shapeless. She was plain. She was ordinary. She was nondescript. She was average.

She wasn't beautiful. But she was Beautiful in every way. She was patient. She was kind. She was gentle. She was loving. She was giving. She was joyful. She was helpful. She made every girl in her Sunday school class feel precious and beloved. She had the mindset and attitude of Jesus.

The old saying — beauty is only skin deep — is true in many ways. The world's idea of beauty has to do with skin. God's idea of Beauty has to do with Skin. And Beauty, unlike beauty, is freely and equally available to everyone.

Some believe that the best way to deal with some girls' skin crises is to reassure us that we're all equally beautiful. They would like us to believe that if you lined up two thousand random girls in a row, each would be as beautiful as all the others. A generous idea — but not at all true. Not if we're talking about skin-deep beauty, anyway. Let's be honest — some people are more beautiful on the outside than others. This isn't a bad thing, and this shouldn't make anyone feel inferior. It's just the way it is. It would be foolish to say everyone is equally tall (or short), equally athletic, equally musical, equally intelligent, and so on. Everyone is different. And that means we all have different degrees of outer beauty. *But it's okay that some people are more skin-deep beautiful than others because skin-deep beauty doesn't determine someone's Skin-deep Beauty.*

Here's the reality — if you believe your value lies solely in beauty, and if you're constantly comparing yourselves to other people's skin, then you'll probably find yourself in a serious skin crisis that will eventually morph into a Skin crisis. The problem doesn't lie with beauty itself. The problem lies with what kind of value we give to beauty. And today's culture, unfortunately, places high value on beauty . . . and not much value on Beauty. God's view is opposite (as is so often the case — have you noticed how God's truth and our culture's "truth" are often completely different from each other?).

Don't get me wrong: I believe it's absolutely fine for girls to pay attention to their outer appearances. It's good to take care of your skin, to be clean (not everyone lives in a place where they can shower every day, or even every week, so don't take it for granted), and to be well-groomed (as my grandmother used to call it). It only makes sense to take care of your physical body since God made it, and since it's the only one you'll ever have in this lifetime, and since keeping it healthy and well maintained (wow . . . that sounds like car talk) makes it possible for you to do God's work. And using makeup, doing your hair, and wearing jewelry in order to "look good" isn't bad, either . . . *unless* you count on those things to raise your value and to make you Beautiful.

One of the world's boldest — and falsest — claims is that being beautiful will make you happy. It won't. Period. End of discussion.

How do I know this? Because there are hundreds of beautiful — and unhappy — people. One of God's boldest claims is that being Beautiful will make you joyful. It will. Period. End of discussion.

Because beauty — a skin-deep measure of outer appearance — can never hold a candle to Beauty — a Skin-deep measure of inner character.

Miss Rau was only one of countless unbeautiful Beautiful people I've known in my lifetime. And what I've come to realize is that, over time, Beauty starts to have an impact on beauty. Outer beauty never makes someone inwardly Beautiful. But inner Beauty very often makes someone outwardly beautiful. I can't really explain why. There's a certain attitude — a certain look, a certain grace, a certain glow (sorry, that sounds so grandmotherly again — but grandmothers can be awfully wise people) that hovers around a Beautiful person. When that happens, the importance of beauty decreases.

Everyone knows how to define *beauty* — it's plastered all over magazine covers and television ads and movie trailers.

But how do you define Beauty? What *is* Beauty?

First, it's not "outward." Height, weight, skin, hair, nose, eyes, feet, ears, shape — they're not Beauty. Second, it's not dependant on specific circumstances or external accessories. What I mean is, even the most beautiful person has lots of off days and moments. The tabloids have a heyday printing non-beautiful pictures of beautiful people — wearing an unflattering outfit, having a bad hair day, without makeup, whatever. (It's sad how much pleasure we get out of seeing a beautiful person looking non-beautiful; I suppose that's because there's so much jealousy and petty competition — among females, especially — to compare our-

2

selves to others and be secretly happy when someone gets taken down a notch or two.) But Beautiful people don't have the same kind of "off" days that are featured in tabloids. Their Beauty is constant and continuous and unwavering. It helps them get through difficult days, and keeps them focused on God and others instead of themselves. That's not to say they're perfect. No one is. But Beautiful people have something that runs deep — much more than skin deep — that positively affects their speech and actions and attitudes. Third, beauty fades with time. But Beauty gets more Beautiful with time. All the age-defying cream in the world won't preserve beauty, but Beauty doesn't require age-defying cream. It's timeless. It's ageless.

It's ... indescribable.

A Deeper Look at Beauty

A lot of my favorite literary female heroes are unbeautiful: Meg in *A Wrinkle in Time*; Vicky in *A Ring of Endless Light*; Anne in *Persuasion*; Jane in *Jane Eyre*; Hari in *The Blue Sword*; Lucy in The Chronicles of Narnia; Nicola in *Queen's Own Fool*; Katherine in *The Perilous Gard*; Matilda in *Matilda Bone*; Birle in *On Fortune's Wheel*; Lucy in *The Ballad of Lucy Whipple*; Louise in *Jacob Have I Loved*; Mattie in *Fever 1793*; Aerin in *The Hero and the Crown*; and many, many more. And they all go through some kind of Skin crisis, during which they learn about themselves, overcome a challenge or problem, grow more confident and courageous, and eventually become — *ta-da!* — Beautiful.

It's not that way in lots of stories. Especially in the movies and bestsellers today, the heroine either starts out beautiful at the beginning, or else she's transformed from ugly duckling to beauty along the way. But the transformation to Beauty is far more compelling and lasting, and makes for a much better story, in my opinion.

Here are some of the things that make my favorite female heroes Beautiful:

- They don't let other people's criticisms discourage them (and most of them are either outcasts or wallflowers or nontraditional girls who get criticized plenty).

- They don't let failure discourage them (and most of them fail plenty of times before they actually find the things they're passionate about and good at).

- They don't let their outer appearances define them (and most of them have plenty of disappointing outer characteristics).

- They eventually believe they have valuable things to offer, no matter how seemingly small or insignificant (and most of them end up doing things that wouldn't be impressive at all in today's media-crazed world, except for Aerin, who kills dragons, which is pretty impressive no matter when or where you live).

- They all believe that inner character and integrity matter more than outer appearance or popularity or success (and most of them are surrounded by more than a few people who believe the opposite).

- They are keenly aware of other people and work hard to honor and please those who should be honored and pleased (and most of them waste no time at all trying to impress or seek shallow acceptance from the Popular Crowd).

- They don't wallow in self-pity because other people are more beautiful, more rich, more famous, more successful (and most of them know plenty of beautiful, rich, famous, and successful people).

That's just for starters.

All of those attributes are positive, and all of them play a part in making someone Beautiful.

But ultimately what defines real Beauty is this: Loving God and loving other people. It's that simple. When you love God and love other people, you live a Beautiful life — you do and say Beautiful things — you *are* Beautiful.

Real Beauty doesn't look the same in every person — sometimes it's outgoing, sometimes it's shy; sometimes it's loud, sometimes it's quiet; sometimes it's artistic, sometimes it's intellectual; sometimes it's emotional, sometimes it's factual. There's lots of room for variety and uniqueness in Beauty. It's not like beauty, which is pretty narrowly defined. Instead, it welcomes all kinds of personalities, all kinds of talents and abilities, all kinds of interests, and all kinds of appearances . . . as long as they love God and love other people.

Beauty and God

From the time I was old enough to look at pictures, read books, and be aware of the world around me, I wanted to be beautiful. What girl doesn't? I wanted to be Cinderella — or any other princess who lives happily ever after. I wanted to be the homecoming queen — or any other girl who's voted "most beautiful." I wanted to be the face on the cover of the yearbook — or any other girl who was fantastically photogenic and gorgeous.

But somewhere during my own Skin crisis, and somewhere along the journey of life, I came to the realization that, as nice as it would be to be beautiful, I would rather be Beautiful. After all there was only so much I could control about beauty. But being Beautiful — well, there's no limit to how Beautiful a girl can be, especially if she's following God and living for Jesus.

Being Beautiful doesn't guarantee happiness. It doesn't guarantee success. It doesn't mean everything will suddenly be awesome and amazing and trouble-free.

Being Beautiful is so very different from being beautiful. It's about *being*, not about *looking*. It's about *attitude and action*, not about *appearance*. It's about *deep joy*, not about *momentary happiness*.

The world says beauty is where it's at, but God says Beauty is where *God's* at ... Beauty surrounds God ... Beauty is part of who God is.

> "One thing I ask from the LORD,
> this only do I seek;
> that I may dwell in the house of the Lord
> all the days of my life,
> to gaze on the beauty of the Lord
> and to seek him in his temple."
>
> *Psalm 27:4*

How can the Lord be Beautiful if God doesn't have a body? God is Beautiful because Beauty has nothing to do with a physical body. It has to do with Skin. And Jesus, who had no "beauty or majesty" in his outer appearance (Isaiah 53:2) was most certainly the most Beautiful and Majestic human who ever walked the earth.

You — no matter who you are and no matter what you look like — can be Beautiful too. And pursuing Beauty is one of the best ways you can work through your personal Skin crisis. Maybe it's time to focus less on beauty products and focus more on Beauty *process* ... becoming more and more like Jesus as you love God and love others.

Going More than Skin Deep:

1. How does the world define *outer beauty*?
2. How would you define *real Beauty*?
3. Think about some Beautiful people you've known. What made or makes them Beautiful?
4. What are some things you can start doing right now to be more Beautiful?

chapter
7

Fashion

Clothe yourselves with the Lord Jesus Christ.
— Romans 13:14

Since God chose you to be the holy people he
loves, you must clothe yourselves with tender-
hearted mercy, kindness, humility, gentleness, and
patience. — Colossians 3:12, *NLT*

Be dressed ready for service and keep your lamps
burning, like servants waiting for their master to return from a wedding banquet. — Luke 12:35–36

That is why I tell you not to worry about everyday
life — whether you have enough food and drink, or
enough clothes to wear. Isn't life more than food,
and your body more than clothing?
— Matthew 6:25, *NLT*

And I want women to be modest in their appearance. They should wear decent and appropriate
clothing and not draw attention to themselves by the
way they fix their hair or by wearing gold or pearls or
expensive clothes. For women who claim to be devoted to God should make themselves attractive by
the good things they do. — 1 Timothy 2:9–10, *NLT*

"No matter what the style or cut of her clothes, the
real woman is always modest and unassuming, with
nothing in her manners or the way she is dressed
that will lower the conception of true womanhood
in the minds of those who see her." (from *Beautiful
Girlhood*, 1922)

A FEW YEARS AGO, ONE OF MY FRIENDS, BETHANY, WAS NOMINATED
to be a freshman princess for the Snowball royal court at her high
school in Minnesota. (Snowball is the winter equivalent of Homecoming
and is named after the crazy-long winter season up north.) Bethany was
known for her eclectic, independent, and unique style. It didn't matter to
her what fashions were featured on the covers of magazines, what the
malls were displaying in the storefronts, what other people were wearing,
or what the fashion experts were hailing as the next trend in clothing.

Bethany wore what Bethany wanted to wear.

And it was usually very different from what other people were
wearing.

There were several nominees for freshman princess, several for soph-
omore princess, several for junior princess, and even more for senior
queen. So there were a grand total of fourteen girls adorned in their
finest dresses, finest shoes, and finest jewelry, along with fancy hairdos,
fancy nails, and fancy makeup. The guys — no surprise — were all wearing exactly the same thing: white tuxes and white shoes rented from

the local bridal shop. (Isn't it weird how guys don't mind wearing the same thing, but most girls would completely flip out if they showed up at Snowball coronation wearing the same dress?)

The girls' dresses were all über elegant — some sequined, some satin; some mermaid-tight, some full-skirted; some strapless, some off the shoulder; some with princess necklines, some with plunging necklines (a few plunging WAY TOO LOW, I might add); some with no waistlines, some with high waistlines; some in black, some in white, some in vivid colors.

And then there was Bethany.

She wore a long pink-and-black plaid skirt, gathered full around the waist, that she'd found at a thrift store some time earlier (she'd been waiting anxiously for a reason to wear it), a matching pink tank top that she'd picked up at a discount store, and a pair of flip-flops. For accessories, she tied a wide pink ribbon around her waist and made a necklace by slipping a simple pendant onto a piece of thin black ribbon. Her curly blonde hair was pulled back into a clip, and she wore as much makeup as she usually did, which was none at all.

Bethany was certainly the least sophisticated looking of all the other female attendants, most of whom were wearing new, sleek, chic designer dresses, along with high, strappy shoes and shiny gold or silver jewelry. Along with their fancy updos and elegant makeup, it looked as though they and Bethany had dressed for different events.

Bethany didn't dress to impress. Bethany didn't dress to make a statement. Bethany didn't dress to be like everyone else.

Bethany dressed to be Bethany — to be fun, modest, unique — to be herself. Bethany dressed the way she did because she knew herself well and because she was comfortable in her own Skin (and skin). At one point I overheard another girl say to her, "You're seriously not going to wear *that*, are you?" To which Bethany smiled and said, "Of course I am. I *love* this skirt!"

Bethany — who didn't fit the status quo mold, who didn't focus on skin, who didn't feel the need to dress a certain way to be accepted or included — was eventually chosen as the freshman princess. In the official Snowball court portrait, she's surrounded by white tuxedos and prom-bridal dresses. She sticks out ... but not like a sore thumb. She sticks out as a person who's confident, joyful, content, unique, and fashionable in her own wonderful way.

Fashion in Context

There are some interesting fashion tidbits in the Bible. Let's start with Eve, who went from naked to figleaf to animal skin. Those are some serious fashion changes in one's own lifetime, wouldn't you say? Then there's Joseph, who traded his shepherd's clothing for a gorgeous coat of many colors. Samson once offered a contest prize that included thirty linen robes and thirty sets of festive clothing (apparently some people had pretty hefty wardrobes, even back then). Rebekah, Joseph's grand-mother, told her favorite son to dress in his brother's clothes in order to trick their dad. Daniel wore a purple robe. John the Baptist wore a tunic made of camel hair (super itchy, for sure). And before Jesus was cruci-fied, the Roman soldiers made bets and divided up his clothing. Fashion has been around a long time.

Today, it's a huge industry in our culture. It's what fills most of the magazines. There are always front-page stories promising new fashion tips, new fashion trends, and new fashion secrets, all of which will magically and instantly make you more happy, more fabulous, and more awesome.

Uh-huh.

Indeed.

Whatever.

The Case Against Bikinis

For those of you who own and wear bikinis, I want you to consider the following case against them:

1. Bikinis are intended to cover as little and expose as much skin as possible. This is an acceptable and lovely thing for your private, married life (which likely none of you has yet), but until then, it's totally, absolutely, one hundred percent contrary to the concept of biblical modesty.
2. Bikinis cover less than most underwear, and since you don't wear your underwear in public, you shouldn't wear a bikini in public.
3. Bikinis—whether you're willing to admit it or not—are at least partially intended to catch the eyes of male onlookers. Therefore they turn your body into an object, cheapen your worth as a human being, and devalue your body as a creation of God.
4. Bikinis—based on number three above—mock God's instructions to avoid lust and temptation and to pursue sexual purity. If you dress in a way that intentionally calls attention to your body, and in the process cause some guys to struggle with lust and temptation, then you're essentially making it difficult or even impossible for them to follow God's word.

My friend, Emi, is the wisest beach-fashionista I know. Whether she's at a pool or a beach, she wears athletic shorts and a short-sleeved surfing shirt. She keeps herself covered, but not ridiculously, and not from head to toe. She never has to worry about whether her outfit will fall off while playing water dodge ball or going down a zipline or waterskiing. She never has to question her motives about trying to attract guys' eyes. She never has to worry about exposing parts of herself that aren't intended for exposure in public. And Emi isn't some weird, backward girl. When she gets married next month, she'll be wearing a gorgeous, sleeveless, princess wedding dress.

Here's a question for you: How much time do you spend picking out your clothes on a typical school day? Do you ever try on outfit after outfit after outfit, trying to find the perfect one that's going to make life good that day? Do you spend significant time in front of the mirror, looking this way and that way, deciding whether or not an outfit makes you look good/thin/pretty/fill in the blank? Do you ever obsess over your fashion style and your closet contents?

And how about this: How much money do you spend on your clothes? More than you give to your church? More than you spend on Jesus?

Teenage magazines regularly feature T-shirts that cost more than twenty dollars, jeans that cost more than sixty dollars, jackets that cost more than seventy dollars, skirts that cost more than eighty dollars, and prom dresses that cost more than two hundred dollars.

Twenty dollars for a T-shirt?! Sixty dollars for jeans?! Two hundred dollars for a special dress?!

If you spend a lot of time picking out your clothes each day, a lot of time shopping for clothes at the mall, or a lot of money buying your clothes, it may be time for you to rethink the role that fashion plays in your life — even if you have the time and cash.

I'm pretty positive that God doesn't want clothes to be one of our top priorities, either for our own self-image or for how we judge others. In fact, God warns about this in the book of James 2:1 – 4 (*NLT*):

> My dear brothers and sisters, how can you claim to have
> faith in our glorious Lord Jesus Christ if you favor some
> people over others?

For example, suppose someone comes into your meeting [or club or school or youth group] dressed in fancy clothes and expensive jewelry, and another comes in who is poor and dressed in dirty clothes. If you give special attention and a good seat to the rich person, but you say to the poor one, "You can stand over there, or else sit on the floor" — well, doesn't this discrimination show that your judgments are guided by evil motives?

Fashion and clothing and style, while not bad things in and of themselves, seem to be pretty low on the list of things God thinks we should focus on.

A Little Fashion Story

I come from a family of garage-sale, thrift-store nutcases. (I say *nutcases* lovingly, of course, since I'm one myself!) I can't remember the last time I bought a new piece of clothing. There are a few reasons for this: 1) The mall gives me a headache (I know — I'm practically non-female in this sense). There are just way too many stores to visit, and in each store there are way too many things to pick from, and among all the things to pick from there are way too many things that either I don't like or won't fit me; 2) I don't like to pay more for my clothing than I have to pay for a hamburger, or a gallon of gas, or a game of bowling. In my opinion it's just crazy to spend that kind of money on something I'll either get tired of or will go out of style in less than two or three years — or even sooner. (Have you noticed how some stores put the season and year on their clothing tags? I believe it's so frequent buyers are reminded that it's time to purchase something new because "this here pair of jeans is *sooo* last season!")

Don't misunderstand me: It's not wrong to buy new clothes. But I believe it's important to remember that every penny you and I have is really God's money, which means we're responsible for spending it wisely and carefully. An expensive coat that will last for many years seems like a reasonable purchase; but an expensive T-shirt destined for the don't-want-it-anymore-pile in a few months seems (excuse me) stupid. And careless.

It's not that God doesn't care about clothing or fashion at all — he does.

In terms of actual clothing and fashion, God cares that it's a reflection of him. In other words, since you are created in the image of God, everything that you do, say, think, *and wear* should present an accurate image of God and God's truth. That means that grace and modesty and wisdom should be more important to you while you pick out clothes than the actual color, style, and fit of the clothes. I'm totally serious about this. When I see what lots of young women are wearing, I'm embarrassed for them. It's not that I believe there should be a set of stringent Fashion Rules, such as:

- Skirts must be this many inches below the knee.
- Necklines must be this many inches above the bustline.
- Waistbands must be this many inches above the hips, etc.

I don't believe God wants us to run around like mad females with tape measures in our hands, squawking at each other that we're one inch too short there and two inches too high there.

But I do believe there are some general guidelines for modesty that every Christian woman and girl should consider. Unfortunately, many of us have fallen prey to the lie that says, "Hey, they're just clothes. No big deal. Lighten up." I've talked to thousands of teenage guys and trust me — they notice the way you dress (which most girls know, and that's exactly why they dress the way they do). Many guys have told me that the hardest part of trying to be godly men with pure hearts in today's culture is dealing with the clothes girls wear: "I try not to notice or stare or pay attention. But seriously ... it's almost impossible sometimes," they say.

I believe your clothes should:

- not be intentionally sexy (you know exactly what I'm talking about).
- not be intended to entice a guy's eyes.
- not be intended to "flaunt it if you've got it."
- not be clothing you'd be embarrassed to wear standing in front of Jesus (a little tricky since none of us knows exactly what this is like, but would you really feel comfortable standing face-to-face and eye-to-eye with Christ in some of the clothes you own or have seen?).

- not be something that says, "Please, please, look at me — you're going to like what you see."

When I was in high school, there weren't too many fashions that were embarrassingly immodest. Plus, we had a dress code at my public school.

But today it can be a challenge to find clothes that are fun, funky, unique, *as well as* appropriate and modest. And for someone who follows Jesus, "appropriate and modest" should be the first criteria you pay attention to, with everything else taking a back seat.

Everything I've shared so far has to do with our culture's concept of fashion, with skin, and with outer clothes. But there's more to fashion than that. There's more to clothes than just plain old clothes. There's also Clothes, apparel for your Skin, Fashion that is God-designed and God-made and God-styled.

I encourage you to stop thinking (and worrying) about what you're going to wear on your skin and start thinking (and praying) about what you're going to wear on your Skin. I'm serious. If we would all spend as much time on our Skin outfits as we do on our skin outfits, well, I can't even begin to imagine what the world would be like.

Here's what the Bible says about Skin Clothing:

> Clothe yourselves with the Lord Jesus Christ.
>
> *Romans 13:14*

> Since God chose you to be the holy people he loves, you must clothe yourselves with tenderhearted mercy, kindness, humility, gentleness, and patience.
>
> *Colossians 3:12, NLT*

> [A woman of noble character] is clothed with strength and dignity.
>
> *Proverbs 31:25*

> And all who have been united with Christ in baptism have put on Christ, like putting on new clothes.
>
> *Galatians 3:27, NLT*

My soul rejoices in my God. For he has clothed me with garments of salvation and arrayed me in a robe of his righteousness.

Isaiah 61:10

Clothes versus clothes

The Clothing that we should wear on our Skin — on our souls and on our hearts — can't be bought in a mall or seen in a magazine or viewed on a shopping network or ordered online. It's not classified as flirty, fun, preppy, goth, or retro. It's not the kind of outfit you wear once a week or once a month or until you get tired of it and buy something new. It's so much more than that. It's real and eternal and sacred.

The world probably wouldn't consider any of it very fashionable. After all, it doesn't do anything to accentuate your bone structure or downplay your hips or add pizzazz to your style. For just a minute, forget the T-shirts, jeans, belts, vests, jackets, skirts, dresses, and blouses. Instead, think about these pieces of Clothing:

mercy
kindness
compassion
humility
salvation
righteousness
the presence and power of Jesus himself

That's a wardrobe that won't put a crimp in your budget ... though it will cost you. Becoming a Christian is free, but following Jesus is costly.

Being clothed in mercy means you can't be worried about getting payback anymore. It means you're willing to forgive, to let bygones be bygones, and to give people a second chance.

Did you know that in the biblical story of Ruth, a sandal was used to seal a real estate deal? It's true.

"Now in those days it was the custom in Israel for anyone transferring a right of purchase to remove his sandal and hand it to the other party. This publicly validated the transaction." — Ruth 4:7, NLT

Jesus' first miracle took place at a wedding ceremony. In the middle of the reception, the wine ran out. So Jesus told some servants to fill six huge stone jars with water, which he then changed into wine. Those huge stone jars were usually filled with water that was used to wash people's dirty feet when they arrived at the party—remember, everyone wore sandals back then, and the streets were dusty, not paved. All that foot dust and dirt had to get washed off somewhere.

Being clothed in kindness means you can't ignore the person who sits alone at lunch every day, the girl who walks alone in the hall, the kid who no one notices, or your sibling who drives you nuts. It means you go out of your way to love them the way Jesus loves you.

Being clothed in compassion means you can't turn your back on the hurting and needy people in your school and community anymore. It means you give your time, and maybe go without certain things, in order to serve and care for those who no one else serves and cares for.

Being clothed in humility means you take off your pride and replace it with something focused on others more than on yourself. It means you no longer consider yourself number one, and you no longer strive to make sure you're the center, the first, the most, the best.

Being clothed in righteousness means you give up the things in your life that aren't pleasing to God. Yes, God is loving and forgiving; but the Bible is clear that being the recipient of God's mercy is no excuse to continue sinning. (By the way, the righteousness we clothe ourselves in isn't our own righteousness; it's the righteousness of Jesus, the sinless, perfect savior of the world.)

Being clothed in Jesus Christ means, well, being clothed in Jesus Christ. It means that when people look at you, they see Jesus. It means *not* being clothed in self, which is what comes naturally to most of us. It means being selfless instead of self-centered. It means starting each day by putting Jesus on, head to toe, top to bottom, one hundred percent. It means that your personal style is Jesus, through and through.

In some ways all of these Clothes are one-size-fits-all. That is, anyone who follows Jesus has access to this wardrobe. But in other ways, all of these Clothes are uniquely fitted to each one of us. Kindness, humility, and compassion might look different for each person, depending on your families, communities, schools, friends, and individual situations.

Here's the bottom line on Fashion: If you want to survive your Skin crisis, you need to dress for success. In terms of clothes, that means being modest and wise. In terms of Clothes, that means filling the closet of your soul with outfits God desires — kindness, compassion, humility, and more. But even more importantly, it means not leaving those outfits tucked away on some spiritual hanger where no one can see them, but instead putting them on each day so that your Skin is ready to face the world, fully clothed.

Going More than Skin Deep:

1. Take time to go through your closet and decide if some of your outfits are immodest. If you're not sure, ask your mom, an aunt, a female youth worker, or another woman you trust. Bite the bullet and get rid of the clothes you shouldn't be wearing.
2. Consider whether you have a bathing suit issue you need to address. If so, now's the time to get serious about it. Start looking for other options if necessary.
3. Look back at the list of Clothes you're supposed to wear on your Skin. Which ones are missing from your wardrobe? How and where are you going to get them?

chapter
8

Shoes

My steps have held to your paths; my feet have not stumbled. — Psalm 17:5

He makes me as surefooted as a deer, enabling me to stand on mountain heights. — Psalm 18:33, *NLT*

He lifted me out of the slimy pit, out of the mud and mire; he set my feet on a rock and gave me a firm place to stand. — Psalm 40:2

"Everyone who calls on the name of the Lord will be saved." How, then, can they call on the one they have not believed in? And how can they believe in the one of whom they have not heard? And how can they hear without someone preaching to them? And how can anyone preach unless they are sent? As it is written: "How beautiful are the feet of those who bring good news!" — Romans 10:13–15/ Isaiah 52:7

Dᴵᴰ ʏᴏᴜ ᴋɴᴏw ᴛʜᴀᴛ Sᴀᴋs Fɪꜰᴛʜ Aᴠᴇɴᴜᴇ ɪɴ Nᴇw Yᴏʀᴋ Cɪᴛʏ ʜᴀs an entire floor devoted just to shoes? Call me crazy ... but that seems a little, well, crazy.

Like many other girls, I own too many shoes. That's partly because, if you remember from the last chapter, I'm a thrift-store queen, so when I see a good pair of shoes priced at $2.99, I usually buy them. Even so, I have about twenty-three fewer pairs of shoes than lots of my friends. I like shoes (*comfortable* shoes) but I'm not a shoe freak like some people. Let's just say I'm pro-shoes (they're a basic necessity, after all, in most places) without being Pro-Shoes.

I think a guy's life, in terms of shoes, would be much easier. My husband has one pair of black dress shoes that he wears for every fancy occasion. I have black dress shoes too ... but not just one pair. I have heels for fancy-schmancy events. I have flats for fancy-casual outfits. I have sandals for fancy-summer attire. And I have other colors besides black because, even though it supposedly goes with everything, it doesn't always *go* with everything, if you know what I mean.

Where do you suppose our love affair with shoes came from in the first place? In the Bible, all you read about are sandals. I don't think they had a huge choice of sandal colors — probably just light tan, medium tan, dark tan, and maybe (for special occasions) black. My grandmother grew up in Norway and each spring she and her siblings had to go into the woods and pick enough berries to each earn money for a new pair of shoes, their *only* pair of shoes. True story. Maybe it all started when women stopped wearing long dresses and their shoes suddenly became visible. Maybe that's when we started thinking that we needed a different pair of shoes for each season, each occasion, in each color of the rainbow.

A September 2009 teen magazine featured 173 pairs of shoes in ads and photo spreads — one being a pair of sneakers available at Macy's for ninety dollars a pair, and another being a pair of ankle high boots designed by Carlos Santana, costing just under one hundred and fifty dollars. An April 1961 issue of the same magazine featured forty-seven pairs of shoes in ads and photo spreads — one being the newly popular white Ked canvas shoe, and another being an orange, open-sided flat, available at Bloomingdale's in New York City for — gasp! — eight whole dollars a pair. (More than my thrift-store shoes, but a whole lot less than a pair of orange, open-sided flats at Bloomingdale's today.)

One recent ad for black-and-pink canvas sneakers features a girl playing an electric guitar and the phrase, "Live life to create." I think I'll buy those — I mean, I want to be creative. Another ad says, "My life. My world. My decree." Ooooh. Awesome. I'm getting those boots and flats because, well, it *is* my life (it's Jesus' actually, but that's a mere technicality), it *is* my world (it's God's actually, but that's a minor detail), and who *wouldn't* want to decree something? Seriously — if those boots and flats are going to give me independence and power, well then, count me in. Another ad company promises I'll be the cutest if I wear its shoes; another says its shoes will give me an earthy feel (whatever that is); another promises me that low booties will "extend my legs," which I think means "make me look taller"; another promises me that the "sexy peep toe and the skinny high heel" will make my entire body "longer and leaner." (Who doesn't want that? And by the way, isn't it a little sad that the peep toe of a shoe can be sexy?!)

You get the idea.

Shoes, says the world, will make me cute, earthy, sexy, longer, leaner, creative, and pretty much perfect.

Shoes might make me appear taller (if the heel is high enough); might keep my feet cool in the summer (if they're sandals); might make my feet hurt (if the toes are too tight or the arch is too flat); might give me blisters (if they don't fit right); might make my feet smell (if they're made out of some strange synthetic leather that doesn't breathe); might make me break my ankle (if the heel is high enough to make me appear taller); might make my heels get all dry and chapped (if they have a rough footbed and I don't wear socks). But they will *not* make my life better, end of story, no matter what the ads or photos tell me.

I don't think God is anti-shoe. I'm positive Jesus wore the standard shoe of his time — sandals — and that he never once apologized for them or worried about whether they would corrupt him. But I also think God might consider it a bit silly and over-the-top to own so many shoes that they have to be categorized and organized by season, style, and color.

I think God cares about feet way more than about shoes — cares about where feet can go and what feet can do. And I think God's ideas and thoughts about feet can go a long way toward helping you survive a Skin crisis. Honest.

Where Feet Go

The Psalms talk a lot about where our feet can take us, both good and bad. Those who don't follow God, who are caught up in themselves, and who let a Skin crisis take their eyes off Jesus, face a pretty tough road. They walk in the way of the wicked (Psalm 1:1) and they walk about in darkness (Psalm 82:5). Their feet lead them in a direction that doesn't lead to God, doesn't lead to obedience, and doesn't lead to joy. Of course, even Christians sometimes have to walk in dangerous places. Psalm 23 says that even if you have to walk through the valley of the shadow of death — meaning the most discouraging, most difficult, most frightening, most awful situation — God is right there close beside you. He does not make you walk alone.

Those who follow Jesus and keep their eyes on him walk in his truth (Psalm 86:11), walk according to his word (Psalm 119:1), walk in his ways (Psalm 119:3), walk in freedom (Psalm 119:45), walk in the way of understanding (Proverbs 9:6), walk humbly (Micah 6:8), walk in the light (1 John 1:7), and walk in love (2 John 1:6). (Different versions of the Bible use different wording. Some read "walk," others read "live," and others read "follow.") How can you get your feet walking in the right direction? One of the best ways is to spend time reading your Bible. It's a lamp to guide your feet and to light your path. (See Psalm 119 for an amazing description of everything God's word is for us.) The more you know about God's plan for your life and the more you know about Jesus — the person we should model our lives after — the more likely you are to walk in the right direction. If you ignore God's word and you ignore the life of Jesus, and then try to live your life wisely, it's like heading on a serious road trip without bringing a map along — or without ever having even looked at a map at all. It's foolish. It's impossible.

The Bible is very clear that when we follow Christ, we should walk in a new way and in a new direction. "Put to death, therefore, whatever belongs to your earthly nature: sexual immorality, impurity, lust, evil desires and greed, which is idolatry. Because of these, the wrath of God is coming. *You used to walk in these ways, in the life you once lived.* But now you must also rid yourselves of all such things as these: anger, rage, malice, slander, and filthy language from your lips.... You have taken off your old self with its practices and have put on the new self, which is being renewed in knowledge in the image of its Creator" (Colossians 3:5 – 10, italics mine).

Ultimately, our feet can take us in only one of two directions — either toward God or away from him. Closer to Jesus or farther from him. Each decision we make is like a step, taking us toward or away, closer or farther. In terms of your Skin, it doesn't really matter what shoes are on your feet — it only matters where your Feet are taking you.

What Feet Can Do

The most obvious thing feet do is take us places. In the case of Skin, they take us to or from God. But they do more than just take *us* to *places* (either good or bad) — they can also be used to bring *things* to *people*.

And the Bible says that the best thing your feet can bring to people is the truth about him. You have to think metaphorically here. Your feet aren't actually going to carry truth. (My feet can't carry anything; they don't have opposable thumbs after all.) But your feet are going to carry you, and you are going to carry and deliver the truth about who Jesus is and what he's done for all people everywhere.

Some of you are probably thinking, "No way. I am not interested in having my feet carry me to some backwoods, undeveloped, dirty, unsanitary place to tell people about Jesus." Others of you are thinking just the opposite and secretly desire to bring the news of Jesus to a faraway, forsaken, forgotten place. The distance and the location don't really matter. You can bring the news to your family. To your friends, your school, your community. And you don't have to have a sermon ready, or stand on a corner shouting into a microphone, or spout off Bible verses all the time in order to bring good news. In fact, these aren't usually very good ways at all. You bring good news by living in a way that helps people see Jesus; by being willing and ready to talk about him if someone asks; by not being ashamed of letting people know you live differently because you love and follow Jesus; by being an example of someone who's been changed by the good news.

Jesus isn't here physically on earth anymore, but you are. Together, we are all supposed to be his "hands and feet," meaning we are supposed to do the work that he started when he lived on earth — loving the unlovable, noticing the unnoticed, feeding the hungry, clothing the poor, and telling people about the love of God.

The Bible says, "How, then, can they call on the one they have not believed in? And how can they believe in the one of whom they have not heard? And how can they hear without someone preaching to them? And how can anyone preach unless they are sent? As it is written: 'How beautiful are the feet of those who bring good news!'" (Romans 10:14 – 15).

Did you see that? It says you can have *beautiful feet*! I'm going to be honest here — I've never thought physical feet were very beautiful. Crooked toes, chapped heels, calluses, blisters, weird bones ... I mean, let's be honest. Feet rarely top the list of someone's Beautiful Body Parts. But Feet — that's another story entirely. If I use my Feet to follow Jesus, to walk in his ways, to walk in the light, to stand firm, and to bring good news to people, well then, Feet can be a very beautiful thing indeed. And even if a Skin crisis is deep and painful and discouraging, there can be great comfort in knowing that through it all, you can still have beautiful Feet.

Going More than Skin Deep:

1. Think about a time when your Feet carried you closer to God and a time when they carried you away from God. What was different about each situation? What things can you do to make sure your Feet carry you in the right direction from now on?
2. Think about who you are — your personality, skills, interests, etc. Where do you think your Feet might lead you in the future?
3. What thing or person makes it hardest for you to keep your Feet on the right path?

chapter
9

Boyfriends and Romance

Girls have more influence with boys than often they realize. (from *Beautiful Girlhood*, 1922)

The "boy problem" is upon you! What are you going to do about it? (from *Girlhood and Character*, 1916)

A one-sided affection is the occupation fever of being a girl, but when it happens to you, you don't care how many other feminine hearts are broken — yours is, and it's devastating! (from *Patterns for Personality*, 1951)

HERE'S A BRIEF OVERVIEW OF MY HISTORY WITH BOYS:
In kindergarten, I loved a boy who smelled like soap and dressed very neatly. I thought if he loved me back, my life would be perfect. He didn't. I survived.

In third grade, I loved a boy who had blue eyes and could make the entire class laugh. I thought if he loved me back, my life would be perfect. He didn't. I survived.

In fifth grade, I loved a boy who was a year older than me and could run very fast. I thought if he loved me back, my life would be perfect. He didn't. I survived.

In seventh grade, I loved a boy who was on the basketball team, was in all the accelerated classes, and was very shy. I thought if he loved me back, my life would be perfect. He didn't. I survived.

In ninth grade, I loved a boy who was a senior in my high school, went to my youth group, and was so manly it took my breath away. I thought if he loved me back, my life would be perfect. He didn't. I survived.

In eleventh grade, I loved a boy who ... you get the idea.

It's a weird thing in today's world — boys are blamed for all kinds of things that girls don't like, but boys are also one of the main objects of attention and affection for girls. Boys are the problem. Boys are the solution. Boys are terrible. Boys are amazing. Boys are annoying. Boys are desirable.

Wow. It all seems a little discombobulated, doesn't it?

I'm a fan of boys. I married one. (A man, actually, but you know what I mean.) I've raised three of my own. I have a boatload of nephews. I happen to think boys are fabulously great.

At the same time, I think the world puts way too much attention and focus on boyfriends and romance as the ultimate problem-solving, make-life-great, everything-will-be-perfect solution to a Skin crisis. Before reading any further, beware. I'm a very conservative person in terms of boys and dating and romance. Some people think I'm old-fashioned, but I'm not. I'm (or at least I try to be) God-fashioned, and trust me — God's ideas about boyfriends and romance are not at all what the world's ideas are.

In our current culture, it's assumed that having a boyfriend is every girl's goal. Even magazines that are geared to older elementary school – aged girls have articles on how to get your crush to notice you, how to tell if he'll be a good kisser (when he finally kisses you, which of course he will, because that's just how it works in the world), and what to say to a guy so he'll like you.

But while the world is glamorizing love, romance, dating, and sex for everyone from teens to adults, the movies, TV shows, and magazines are also filled with stories and articles about "hookup stress," "date-mares," "how to avoid fwb [friends with benefits] troubles," and "the best and quickest way to breakup and move on."

What is going on?! Are boyfriends the magical answer to life, or aren't they? There seems to be a lot of disagreement.

If you've ever watched a chick flick, you know that the moment everyone waits for (or at least the moment most girls wait for) is when, after ninety long minutes — during which the major guy-girl relationship is on, off, on, off, not sure, on, off, trouble ahead, misunderstanding, off for sure, maybe on, mistaken identity, off for *sure* this time — things finally fall into place. After a long chase scene (not the cop-car kind, but the people kind where either the guy or girl chases the other one who is just getting ready to catch a plane, jump into a cab, climb onto a boat, or step into a carriage) the guy and girl stare into each other's eyes. They move closer. Their hands touch. He puts one hand on her face. Their foreheads touch. He delivers a perfectly scripted speech about loving her forever, loving her more than anyone, loving her to the ends of the earth, loving her until the end of time, loving her with his entire heart and soul, loving her more than life itself. And they . . . . kiss. And the credits roll.

The guys at the theater mutter about how "the movies always end the same" and "why did they have to ruin it" and "I sat through ninety minutes for this?" and "Oh, not again." The girls hold their breath, smile secretly, sometimes blink back tears, and whisper, "Oh, if only that were me. *My life would be perfect.*"

At least that's what most of the guys think and what most of the girls do.

Most girls are hardwired in such a way that they are emotionally affected by love stories. Even little girls who watch princess movies and movies about high school musicals are often affected by the romance. Maybe not to the same extent as teen girls, but affected nonetheless.

The world knows this and the world capitalizes on it. Romance is featured in a majority of the ads in teen magazines. There are regular features about "your love life." The Q and A sections are filled with complaints and queries about boys and love and a lack thereof. Almost every television show or movie intended for teen and young adult women features a love story. Even the recent movie based on the book *Prince Caspian* added a romantic storyline and a last-minute kiss that doesn't exist in the book. (You don't think that was accidental, do you? It was intentional, and it was aimed at you.) Guys are rated based on how hot they are. Our vocabulary regularly includes terms like going out, making out, breaking up, making up, hooking up, friends with benefits, hot, babe, fox, hunk, and things I can't write here because they will (or they should) make you blush.

The old saying that "sex sells" is certainly true. But so does romance. And you are the main target.

First off, I don't think love, romance, crushing, guys, and all things related are bad. In fact, many of those things are part of our God-given design. Of course, in a sinful world, the design often gets messed up along the way and something that was intended to be wonderful gets twisted into something that's not at all wonderful and is in fact deceptively dangerous.

In my opinion, one of the most amazing experiences of life is falling in love with someone (and I do believe you can "fall in love" when you're a teen, though it's a very different kind and depth of love than adult married people share). I vividly remember the physical reaction that I had when I was in the same room with, or even thought about, a certain guy I really, really cared about. I could actually feel it in my stomach. The feelings could be caused by something as simple as seeing him down the hallway at school, glimpsing him in the parking lot at church, or hearing his voice as he talked to a friend. The flips and flops and flutters in my gut weren't my imagination. They were real. And they were amazing. Even the memory of a glimpse or a conversation could produce those flips, flops, and flutters. It was part of my biology. I couldn't do a flip in gymnastics class if my life depended on it, but one glimpse of the boy I loved, and watch out world because my stomach would have flipped me across the entire school building if such a thing were possible.

The problem with Hollywood and the media is that they take advantage of many girls' tendency to fall in love and have flip-flop-flutter reactions to romance. They use images, words, music, and storylines to suck you into a fake and false romance, not because they care about you but *because they want your money.* I'm totally serious about this. They won't sell another magazine, book, movie ticket, or ad slot to advertisers if they don't make money. And they won't make money if they can't suck you in. And they won't suck you in unless they know your weak spot. And trust me . . . they know your weak spot.

That might sound really negative and skeptical. It should. I do not for one minute believe that the world has your best interests at heart. The world has its own best interests at heart, and the best way to serve its interests is by controlling you. Stop and think for a moment: How many of your favorite movies are romances? How many of your favorite books are romances? How many of your favorite television shows are about romantic relationships? How many of the magazines you read regularly feature photos and articles about guys and romance?

Romance isn't the enemy here. Romance is a wonderful thing. Rather, fake romance (which is also unrealistic romance, I might add) that is used to control and manipulate you is the enemy. And it's a very formidable enemy, first because it's so prevalent, and second because it's so subtle.

It's easy for people to brush it off as harmless and not worth fighting about. But they're wrong. It *is* a big deal. And it *isn't* harmless. And it *is* worth fighting about (not fist-fighting, but fighting for God's truth). You might be thinking, "Oh my, she's one of those whacked-out, ultra-weird, über-psycho freaks who thinks we should all go to girls' schools, wear long dresses, be nurses and teachers and nuns, and never ever look at boys." Actually, no, I don't. Nor do I think you should try to rid your life of all romantic feelings. I just think you should be aware of the effects of unrealistic romance, which, by the way, is what *all* worldly romance is. Life, you know, is never like the movies. The more fake and unrealistic romance you consume, the more you're going to desire it, and the more disappointed you're going to be when real and good romance comes your way.

Boyfriends and romance, no matter what the magazines or movies say, are not the answer to a Skin crisis. More often than not, they're part of the problem. (Not guys specifically, but the ideas and desires we have about guys.) Girls who want a boyfriend but don't have one feel bad about themselves. Girls who have a boyfriend sometimes feel overly confident for the wrong reasons. Girls who have a boyfriend but whose relationship isn't going well struggle with what to do. Girls who spend a lot of time desiring, thinking about, and pursuing a boyfriend and romance are actually wasting time desiring, thinking about, and pursuing things that *are not* going to solve or lessen a Skin crisis.

Instead of boyfriends and romance, during junior high and high school (and for some of you, even into the first few years of college) you should set your sights on community and love. Here's why.

Boyfriends are a fad, but community is ageless

People today talk about boyfriends, girlfriends, and going out as though they'd been around since the beginning of time. ("What . . . ? Didn't Adam and Eve go out?") But in fact, exclusive dating — going out — is a fairly new social phenomenon, not even a hundred years old. Dating started in the early part of the 1900s, and exclusive dating — "I belong to her, she belongs to me" — really got started during the World War II years. If you want to know how successful and healthy exclusive dating has been, you might want to look around you at the condition of many families and the number of marriages that don't last. Divorce rates have increased right alongside exclusive dating statistics. I think there's a good explanation for that (see the "Boyfriends are temporary, but community is lasting" section that follows). Part of the problem is that the age when people get married has gotten higher, but the desire to be with someone has stayed the same, so instead of courting or getting engaged, lots of teens go out. If you recall from chapter four, in 1961, *Seventeen* magazine was filled with ads for engagement rings. It also had ads for hope chests, china, furniture, and linens, all with soon-to-be-married young women in mind.

The answer isn't for people to start getting married in high school again. High school marriages in today's world have a very low rate of success. And the world has changed so that high school marriages no longer fit into a strong and secure existence. The answer is to focus on something other than romantic relationships, and the best alternative is strong community made up of a group of like-minded, caring, committed friends. Community can be in all sorts of places — immediate families, extended families, school, friends, neighborhoods, and church.

Boyfriends are exclusive, but community is inclusive

When a couple goes out, there are rules about how each person can interact with other people. You're not allowed to like (in the romantic sense) anyone else. You're expected to spend significant time with each other, even if that means not spending time with other friends. You're not supposed to have other really close guy or girl friends. If there's a special event (like a school dance), you're not allowed to go with anyone else. You're supposed to share all your thoughts and feelings with each other. You're supposed to check-in regularly. (Woe to the boyfriend who goes on a family vacation or a road trip with friends and doesn't text or call his girlfriend often enough.) Even though these rules are unspoken, and even though they may not feel restrictive (especially at first, when you're still starry-eyed and gaga over each other), they are still there. And if you think about the "rules" honestly, you'll see that they're really a set of premarital marriage vows: I promise to love only you, I promise to be faithful to you, I promise to be with only you, I promise to ... These are promises and vows that are intended for a lifelong relationship and the step immediately preceding that — engagement.

The ultimate exclusive relationship — marriage — is sacred and holy. It is designed to be a visible and earthly representation of Christ and the church in the depth of its devotion, its commitment, and its love. This is difficult enough for married couples to do. It is not possible — nor is it intended — for unmarried teens to be a representation of Christ and the church.

Community (a group of friends), on the other hand, is meant to be inclusive. When it's not, as in the case of cliques or school sororities, we all know how painful it can be. That is not community the way Christ intended it. Communities are meant to be sources of encouragement, challenge, and support. Though there may be various levels of friendships within a community, there are not rules about who must spend how much time with whom.

Boyfriends are temporary, but community is lasting

Those of you who have boyfriends aren't going to like hearing this, but the fact is that more than nine out of ten high school dating relationships don't last. They end in a breakup that is guaranteed to make at least one person miserable for a period of time. In the almost thirty years that my husband and I have worked with teens, and in the years prior to that when I was a teen myself, I've never known or heard about a couple who broke up and then both said, "Wow ... I feel *absolutely and utterly fantastic*. Seriously. This is the *best* thing that's ever happened to me." At least one person is devastated, hurt, and brokenhearted, sometimes for weeks and months. There is nothing about devastating, hurting, or breaking the heart of another person that reflects the image of God to those around you.

Some people argue that a breakup can teach you important life lessons and that you'll grow stronger through the pain, and that you'll be a better person for having gone through a difficult situation. I think that's rubbish. You have plenty of important life lessons to learn without adding this one. And just because you *can* learn something from a difficult situation doesn't mean you *should*. The Bible says that God works through our trials and difficulties, but that doesn't mean we should knowingly walk into a situation that will result in a trial or difficulty.

Plus, breaking up — which is almost certainly going to happen to someone who goes out in high school — is terrible practice for the rest of life. Think about the reasons people break up with each other:

I don't like him/her anymore.
S/he annoys me.
I like someone else.
I'm bored with him/her.
I need time to myself.
I need more space.
The magic is gone.
I want a change.
We've grown apart.

Those are many of the same reasons that people get divorced. In other words, when you break up with someone, you are practicing a behavior that is totally outside of God's design for a committed relationship. If you break up with someone now because "you're just not that into him anymore," why do you think it will be any different when and if you get married someday? Trust me—married people experience all of the things on the list above, and breaking up isn't an option if they are Christians. The best way to practice faithfulness now is to not make promises you can't keep.

Community, on the other hand—though it goes through changes— does not end in the same way that romance often does, with a breakup. That's because it's not centered around a couple—it's centered around something intangible and unseen, like beliefs, interests, family ties, or values. Even when there are disagreements in a community, and even if some people leave and some people join, the community continues.

Romance is centered around feeling, but love is centered around being and doing

One of the reasons girls love romances is because they stir up strong emotions. But emotions and feelings, as we all know, are fickle. I hate it when people say, "Girls are fickle," but I do think that girls' emotions can often appear fickle. They change like the wind. At this time in your life, adding one more emotionally centered element is dangerous. There are already plenty of things that affect us emotionally. And I'm not saying that romantic emotions are all bad. I'm just saying that giving them free rein, and being in a relationship where they are central, is a bad idea.

Love, on the other hand—and I'm talking about the love of the Bible, the love of 1 Corinthians 13 (you can read more about this in the next chapter)—is far, far above romance (which is love of a different kind) and it takes a long time to develop and learn it. You need to be working on your love skills, not your romance skills.

Let me give you an example.

When my husband, Mark, and I went on our first date—after knowing each other for two years of college, being best friends for most of that time, and being totally caught off guard by romantic feelings — we sat in a two-door, orange (and rusty), standard transmission Ford Fiesta at a local drive-in theater where *Snow White* and *The Black Stallion* were playing as a double feature. (Honest. I couldn't make that up.) It didn't really start out as a date, but it ended up that way. Somewhere in the middle of *Snow White*, when the princess was singing in her high, warbling, and rather annoying voice, Mark reached over, gently and respectfully, and held my hand.

I'm going to tell you the truth — the foundation of my world was totally shaken. I was breathless. I couldn't think straight. I was out of my mind with joy, amazement, and shock. I think a few tears dripped down my cheeks. I mean, it was amazing beyond words. I will never, ever forget that moment. It was very real. It was very beautiful. It was earth-shattering.

And it was based purely on emotion.

After twenty-five years of marriage, there aren't as many earth-shattering moments. It's not because Mark and I don't love each other as much as we did back then. In fact, we love each other much, much more. It's just that you can't live a life that's built on emotion. You need something more solid, more reliable, more true. You need a different kind of love, one that isn't based on romance or passion or desire. It needs to be based on Christ's deep, sincere, sacrificial love. That kind of love — the Bible sometimes translates it as charity — is for all people. And that's the kind of love that God calls you to show to others as a way of reflecting him.

Romance has a sexual component, but love is spiritual and relational

If you have a boyfriend, and you've committed to having a sexually pure relationship, don't get in a huff and skip this section. This is for you too. Most teen sexual activity (and that includes anything that goes beyond intimate kissing, and some people even include that because people who are married don't kiss other people — in other words, it's a marriage activity) happens between people who are going out. Yes, there's tons of stuff that happens between people who aren't a couple, but in high school, a majority of it happens within exclusive dating relationships. As friends, a guy and girl can have a spiritual friendship, an emotional friendship, and an intellectual friendship. So what's the point of going out? One, to belong to each other (bad idea). And two, to have a physical relationship. Even if you've committed to going no further than holding hands or kissing in a romantic relationship, there's always a temptation to do more. (Seriously, anything beyond kissing is totally off limits for people who aren't married. *Totally* off limits. There is no loop hole or technicality that can allow you to do anything else and still be within God's design.) The best way to beat temptation is to avoid it. The best way to avoid it is to eliminate it. If you're going out and you've committed to having a pure physical relationship, then why not consider *not* going out? You can still have a spiritual, emotional, and intellectual relationship. The only thing you'd be eliminating is the possessive element (belonging to each other) and the physical element. If you can't imagine giving up these two things, than you need to seriously reconsider the nature of your romance.

Just a quick note to those of you who are involved in a physical relationship — it's time to make a choice between sexual purity and your relationship with God. I'm not saying that God will dump you if you're sexually impure — God doesn't dump people once they belong to him. But your relationship with God is fractured and can't be its best as long as you willingly live outside his boundaries for you. And as far as "sexually pure" goes, the best definition and guideline I can give you is this: Don't do anything with a guy now that you don't want your future husband to someday do with another woman when he's married to you.

One more quick note to those of you who've been involved in a physical relationship in the past — God's forgiveness is *total, complete, perfect*, and *forever*. If you confess, your Heart and Skin are washed clean. There will still likely be emotional issues, and even possibly physical issues you must deal with, but spiritually, you are pure.

Romance is vague, but love is clearly defined and demonstrated in Jesus

When Mark held my hand in that rusty Ford Fiesta twenty-seven years ago, it was romantic. We were young and newly in love. Today when Mark smiles at me from the opposite end of the cereal aisle at the grocery store while he piles his cart with sugary stuff, it can still be terribly romantic ... or not, depending on the day, how I'm feeling, what we talked about that morning, all kinds of things. Romance is a slippery, vague thing that can't be counted on. It's strange that way. That's one of the things that makes it, well, romantic. It catches you off guard. It surprises you. For those very reasons, it shouldn't be a focal point of life.

The focal point of your life should be the example of Jesus, the way he loved everyone he met and knew, including his close friends, his enemies, and the most unlovable people in all of society. That's what you should be focusing on — loving the way Jesus loved. Being like Jesus. Learning to give yourself sacrificially to those around you, instead of giving yourself exclusively to a boyfriend.

Okay, that was a lot to take in. There's so much more to say about this, but hopefully this is enough to get you thinking.

Here are a few final thoughts.

If you think I'm going overboard on this, taking all this dating, boyfriend, and romance stuff too seriously, then think again. Committed romantic relationships are intended to be serious — which is one of the reasons why junior high and high school aren't a good time for them. I read a story this week about a new celebrity couple, and the woman said, "Yes, it's true — we're dating. But it's not serious." Not serious? Hmmm. Maybe that's the problem — we don't take dating seriously enough. It's just a game. I don't think God considers it a game. There's too much at stake.

If you have a boyfriend, I'm not suggesting that you should call him right now and break up with him. However, I do think you should consider carefully *why* you're going out, what's going to happen when you or he no longer wants to go out (which I'm sure you think will never happen, but statistics say otherwise), how that's going to make one or both of you feel, and how all of that fits into being created in the image of God. In other words, I think you should reconsider the exclusive nature of your relationship (which doesn't mean I think you should start dating lots of different people!). If he's the awesome guy that you think he is, maybe the two of you can have a conversation now and can find a mutually acceptable way to redefine your relationship that makes it neither exclusive nor broken.

If you don't have a boyfriend, I want you to know that you are in a *very good place* at this point in your life. Seriously. Especially if you can see it with a new perspective. Wishing you had a boyfriend and not having one can be awful. One way to ease that pain would be to stop watching/reading/listening to things that make you want a boyfriend. That just feeds the desire. Second, spend more time in community — friends, family, anyone you enjoy being around who loves and supports the real you, the you that's more than skin deep. Having a good time with other people can be more enjoyable than some of the drama that comes with romantic relationships. And in many groups and communities, you can get to know guys as friends, which is the best kind of relationship to have with them right now. Third, find ways that you can use your time to serve other people. You'll realize that the rewards and satisfaction of helping others will help ease your need to feel loved and accepted by a certain guy.

Here's the deal — boyfriends and romance are not going to make your life perfect. They aren't going to solve or eliminate a Skin crisis. They're not going to prepare you for life beyond high school. And they're not, in most cases, going to help you reflect the character of Jesus to people around you. In order to do that, you need community and love.

Going More than Skin Deep:

1. If you have a boyfriend: honestly examine your relationship. What things need to change? What things might not reflect the image of God to people around you? How could you redefine your relationship in a way that's honoring and obedient? (By the way, if your boyfriend isn't a Christian, the relationship absolutely needs to end. Seriously. You cannot possibly reflect Jesus if you've committed yourself to someone who doesn't love him and live for him.)

2. If you don't have a boyfriend: I was you in high school. No one had ever said to me, "Hey, boyfriends aren't necessary." Every message I got was that boyfriends were the norm — even my church started talking about dating as early as junior high, and I was one of the girls without a boyfriend. This is all I want to say to you — take time tonight to be honest about how you feel (whether that's sad, disappointed, angry, lonely, whatever) and then trust and believe that God has your best interests at heart. It's not going to make your longings or desires go away immediately, but I believe God is much more powerful than romantic desires, emotional longings, and relational dreams. He's *God*, for crying out loud!!

chapter 10

Skin Care

Simple Rules for General Appearance:

1. Always keep your hair well groomed.
2. Keep your skin clear and smooth by proper eating, sleeping, and exercise.
3. Wash your face, neck, and ears thoroughly at least once a day with lukewarm water and a mild soap. Scrub your elbows and neck. Wash your nostrils.
4. Cream your face at night to avoid dry skin.
5. Use good judgment in the amount and application of makeup.
6. If you must pluck your eyebrows, trim them only.
7. Don't chew gum in public.
8. Wear sensible shoes and keep them polished.
9. Keep the seams in your stockings straight.
10. Take several baths a week.
11. Your mouth or teeth may offend others unless they are kept clean.

(from *Strictly Confidential*, 1944)

THE OTHER DAY, I STOOD IN THE SKIN CARE AISLE AT MY LOCAL PHARMACY, looking for a face lotion that would moisturize my skin without clogging my pores. (That sounded like a commercial soundbite, didn't it?) I don't spend a lot of time or attention on my face, but every now and then, I realize it's the only one I'm ever going to have in this lifetime and I should spend at least a little bit of time taking care of it.

So there I was, staring at an entire aisle (six shelves high and at least thirty feet long which equals a minimum of 180 square feet) of skin moisturizers. I was paralyzed by the sheer number of options. Nighttime. Daytime. Oil free. With added sunscreen. Fragrance free. With extra vitamins. All natural. Dermatologist tested. Dermatologist approved. Dermatologist recommended. Bestselling. As seen on TV. Only available in stores. Generic brands. For sensitive skin. Anti-aging. Deep wrinkle. Pore reducing. Oil controlling. Acne preventing.

Aaaaaaaaaahhhhhhhhh! My mind went into overload and totally shut down. I had no idea where to start. There were too many labels to read. There were too many ingredients to understand. There were too many claims to sort through. I wanted a clerk to say, "Here, ma'am, this is the perfect moisturizer for you. Trust me." But no one did. So I finally grabbed one (on the left side, eyelevel, in a pleasant green-colored package), balked at the pricetag, bought it anyway, then raced home to the security and serenity of my office (which, by the way, is lined with books, six shelves high, at least thirty feet in length each, which equals a minimum of 180 square feet of books, an amount which *never* gives me a headache, causes my mind to shut down, or prevents me from knowing exactly which book I want to read at any particular moment).

I used the lotion when I got home. My skin didn't feel any different.

I'm sure in a few weeks time, I'll notice a difference — that is, if I use the lotion according to the directions, don't give up after a few days, take the time to wash my face, and do all those other time-consuming things you're supposed to do in a healthy, systematic, devoted skin care regimen.

At least I hope so.

Like we talked about in Chapter 1, while I think skin care is legitimate (remember, God made your face, elbows, ankles, and knees, and you should take care of them), I think Skin care is way more important and usually gets far less attention. Why? Because it's not a commercial product. Because no one can make money off of it. Because you can't photograph it and put it in a magazine layout. Because it's not sexy, stylish, and stunning.

Rather, it's sacred. And spiritual. And soulful.

And, might I add, it's absolutely vital to your eternal health and well-being — both now, during the years when you're quite likely going through one or more Skin crises of your own, and later, when you might be beyond the most serious of your Skin crises but still need to have healthy Skin, soul, and spirit in order to live life to its fullest.

I recently saw an infomercial titled "Serious Skin Care Celebration." It featured a set of skin care products that were guaranteed to make you look and feel younger, or your money back. The products were categorized by age, skin type, and desired results. There weren't quite as many options as I faced at my local pharmacy while shopping for plain old face moisturizer, but there were still plenty to choose from. All the products pretty much fell into one of several categories: cleansers (daily and deep); toners; moisturizers (daily and weekly); and sun-damage prevention. After thinking about it for a while, I think these are perfect categories for Skin care too. And so without further ado, I'd like to present my own version of "Serious Skin Care Celebration," featuring some serious Skin care steps that will cost you nothing in terms of money, but might cost you plenty in terms of commitment, dedication, and desire.

Cleanse

The first and most basic step in any Skin care regime is cleansing — washing away all the grime and gook of life that, if left to its own devices, will block your Skin's pores and cause trouble down the road. When you first gave yourself to Christ and became a Christian, your heart and soul and Skin were immediately and completely washed clean and made pure. Your old self was removed and you were given a new self — a new Skin — that was clothed in the righteousness and purity of Jesus. But, because you are human, there is still a daily struggle with former desires and sinful inclinations, like we talked about in Chapter 3. It is critically important for you to confess those sins and make a clean start each day.

I John 1:9 says, "If we admit our sins — make a clean breast of them — he won't let us down; he'll be true to himself. He'll forgive our sins and purge us of all wrongdoing" (*The Message*). If you aren't sure if or how you've sinned, you might want to pray the words of David from Psalm 139:23 – 24 (*NLT*):

> Search me, O God, and know my heart;
> test me and know my anxious thoughts.
> Point out anything in me that offends you,
> and lead me along the path of everlasting life.

In certain situations, you might need to have other Christian friends to whom you can be accountable. James 5:16 says, "Make this your common practice: Confess your sins to each other and pray for each other so that you can live together whole and healed" (*The Message*). I don't think it's necessary, or even wise, for you to confess each and every sin in front of your entire youth group or small group all the time. That kind of confession can be self-serving, sort of like, "Hey, everyone, you'll never believe how bad I've been!" Confessing — cleansing — isn't meant to be an event in which you advertise and flaunt your failings.

It's meant to be a process that gets rid of the grime and dirt thoroughly, after which the washrag gets tossed in the laundry, the cleansing towel gets thrown in the garbage, or the dirt gets wiped off and rinsed down the drain. It's really quite an amazing thing.

Sin not only affects our relationship with God but also our relationships with other people. So confession not only makes things right with God but it also makes things right with others so that we can live in healthy community. It can take time for forgiveness and healing to take place, but without confession there is very little hope of having healthy Skin. One thing I've observed is that we are often reluctant to confess to the people who are closest to us — our family. Since a Skin crisis often causes relationships with parents to be less than ideal (even awful, sometimes), it's extra important that you not neglect this cleansing step with them. I'm not going to make you a false promise and say that things will automatically be fabulous with your parents. But this is the perfect place to start.

So cleanse, cleanse, cleanse. Every day. Carefully. Thoroughly. Diligently. Faithfully. You'll be glad you did.

Tone

Face toner is a weird thing. Without your skin ever having to do an ounce of work or exert any energy, toner supposedly tightens, firms, and strengthens your skin. Unfortunately, it's not quite that easy with Skin care. There's nothing you can pour on a cotton ball and wipe over your Skin that's going to magically tighten, firm, and strengthen it. In the case of Skin, toning is going to require more exertion on your part. In fact, exercise might be a better description of this step than toning.

What does it mean to have tight, firm, and strong Skin? To have a soul that's in shape? To have a spirit that's toned? I believe it means the same thing as it does in the exercise world. Toned arms can do arms' work easily. Strong legs can do legs' work effortlessly. Toned Skin/spirit/soul are prepared to do the work intended for them — loving God and loving others. This really is the single job of your Skin and everything inside of it.

And it's a very big job.

You can imagine that keeping your Skin toned is going to take way more work than toning your skin, and even more work than toning your abs, thighs, or triceps. It's going to require daily exercise, practice, and workouts. That will probably look different for each person (just like physical exercise does) but it basically involves simply this: using and moving your Skin/soul/spirit in greater amounts for longer lengths of time. It means loving God and loving others — in whatever way you can — a little more and a little bit longer each and every day, until your Skin is so toned that you can love consistently and constantly.

This is how you love others:

- be patient
- be kind
- do not want what you don't have
- do not boast
- do not be proud
- do not be rude
- do not think more highly of yourself than of others
- do not fly off the handle
- do not hold grudges
- do not delight in evil
- rejoice in the truth
- protect, trust, hope, persevere (see 1 Corinthians 13)

There are certainly plenty of things there to work on, and they will all require huge amounts of practice and exercise. Pick one. Pick two.

Pick several. Start doing them today. At home, at school, at work. Each time you do one of those things, you'll be toning your Skin. You'll be strengthening your soul. You'll be firming your spirit. Over time, you'll discover that your spiritual stamina has increased more than you'd ever imagined possible. But be warned: This is not one of those four-week exercise programs. This is lifelong. You never finish this program. You never get to stop and relax and say, "Ah ... finally I'm toned. Time for a break."

This is how you love God:

- by loving others (see the preceding list)
- by worshiping him
- by delighting in his truth
- by obeying him
- by revering him
- by putting him before yourself, always
- by letting him guide you
- by trusting him
- by letting yourself drown in his love for you

These are more about "being" than "doing," (and even though "to be" might sound like less work than "to do," I've found that "being" — if it's done right — often requires more effort and dedication than "doing"). The things in this list are all about attitudes, convictions, and beliefs. They aren't visible or tangible at first. But slowly, over time, they will start to transform you from the inside out so that a new you will emerge, a you that loves God more deeply, more faithfully, and more sincerely.

Toning is hard work in the world of Skin care. I wish it were as easy for Skin as it is for skin, but alas, good things never come easily. But that's why the payoff is so sweet in the end.

Moisturize

If you live up north where the winters are dry and long, or in the desert region, or if you've got naturally dry skin, you know how important it is to moisturize. It gets even more important as you get older. Dry skin is wrinkly skin. Dry skin is unhealthy skin. Dry skin is always in danger of cracking, blistering, and peeling. Skin needs to be moisturized. Every day. Several times. Some experts even recommend using a weekly deep moisturizer in addition to a regular daily moisturizer.

Guess what?

Your Skin needs moisturizer too. Even more than your skin does. If your Skin is dry, it's in danger of cracking under the weight of sorrow, of blistering under the pain of disappointment, and of peeling from the pressures of life. Your Skin needs to be moisturized. Every day. Several times. Some Skin experts — God, for example — even recommend using a weekly deep moisturizer in addition to your regular daily moisturizer.

It's not hard to moisturize, but it takes dedication and commitment. It won't happen on its own. You can't simply imagine your way to moisturized Skin. You have to actually do something, to apply something, to give your Skin the chance to soak up the moisture it needs to stay healthy. How? By soaking up the presence of Jesus and the Word of God.

In the gospel of John, there's a story about Jesus meeting a woman at a well (read John 4:1 – 14). Jesus asked the woman to draw a bucket of water for him, and then said, "If you knew who I was, you'd ask *me* for water, and I would give you living water instead!"

> "Anyone who drinks this water [from the well] will soon become
> thirsty again. But those who drink the water I give will never be
> thirsty again. It becomes a fresh, bubbling spring within them, giving
> them eternal life."
>
> *John 4:13 – 14, NLT*

What water does Jesus give us? Himself. His presence. His love, life, death, resurrection, his example.

Getting to know Jesus happens in a few ways. First, by reading, knowing, and experiencing his story. The main part of his story takes place in the gospels — Matthew, Mark, Luke, and John — but the entire Bible is directly related to Jesus. So anytime you read, meditate on, pray over, and memorize Scripture, you are moisturizing your Skin. In Psalm 1, it says that the person who delights in the law of the Lord — that is, delights in the words of Scripture — and meditates on it day and night is like a tree planted along a riverbank, where its roots can soak up water all day long, staying moisturized. When a tree gets water, its leaves never wither and it bears fruit each season. Likewise, when your Skin has constant access to water — living water, Jesus — it will never wither and it will bear fruit (live a godly life) each season.

Another way to moisturize is to gather with other Christians to worship, rejoice, and be taught more deeply the truths in the Bible. This is your weekly deep-moisturizing step, and it might happen on Sunday morning in church, on Sunday night in small group, on Wednesday night in youth group, or whenever and wherever. The New Testament is full of examples of people gathering around Jesus to hear him teach and watch him minister. In the book of Acts, new Christians gathered to pray, encourage one another, serve others, and worship. Though each individual believer is moisturized in a gathering, it is that much more potent because it's happening in the context of community. The effect is multiplied. Reading, praying, studying, meditating, worshiping, and memorizing need to happen daily in your own private time with God, but they also need to happen throughout the week in your corporate time with God. If you skip this step, your Skin will dry up and be good for nothing.

Protect

Everyone knows that UV rays from the sun are dangerous and damaging for skin. Even people who tan need to be careful — tanned skin is damaged just like burned skin; it just doesn't look as painful.

Your Skin needs to be protected too, from all kinds of things — worldly influences, harmful images, false ideas, deceptive opinions, and so much more. The sun is dangerous, but that doesn't mean people should stay indoors all day. The wise person who heads outdoors to enjoy the fresh air, the sun's warmth, and the beauty of nature wears sunscreen as protection. In the same way, you can't stay indoors your whole life and totally avoid the world (though there are lots of things in the world that you should absolutely avoid). The wise person who heads into the world to enjoy the company of other people, to be a positive influence, and to reflect the love of Christ wears sunscreen as protection.

If only it were that easy. Wouldn't it be amazing if you could walk into a store and buy a jar of WPF 40 (world protection factor) that promised to protect you against all the dangers of sin, evil, and temptation? Apply once in the morning and once at night (and maybe once during the school day, just to be safe) and ta-da! No danger and no damage. Ever.

Of course, that wouldn't require any faith, spiritual growth, or dependence on God. The only hope we have of protecting and guarding ourselves is going to require a lot more effort than spreading a layer of sunscreen on our skin. It's going to require layer upon layer upon layer of protection on our Skin. In his letter to the church in Ephesus, this is how Paul tells Christians to protect themselves from dangerous worldly influences:

> God is strong, and he wants you strong. So take everything the
> Master has set out for you, well-made weapons of the best materials.

And put them to use so you will be able to stand up to everything the Devil throws your way. This is no afternoon athletic contest that we'll walk away from and forget about in a couple of hours. This is for keeps, a life-or-death fight to the finish against the Devil and all his angels.

Be prepared. You're up against far more than you can handle on your own. Take all the help you can get, every weapon God has issued, so that when it's all over but the shouting you'll still be on your feet. Truth, righteousness, peace, faith, and salvation are more than words. Learn how to apply them. You'll need them throughout your life. God's Word is an *indispensable* weapon. In the same way, prayer is essential in this ongoing warfare. Pray hard and long. Pray for your brothers and sisters. Keep your eyes open. Keep each other's spirits up so that no one falls behind or drops out.

Ephesians 6:10 – 18, The Message

There's nothing I can add to that. The Bible is clear:

- Be prepared. Don't be naive about the world.
- Don't try to be strong on your own. You can't do it. You need God and others.
- Apply (like sunscreen!) truth, righteousness, peace, and faith to every situation.
- Spend time in the Word.
- Pray. Pray. Pray.
- Be alert.
- Be in community.

That's the Skin version of sunscreen. Depending on the situation, you might need a higher or lower protection factor. But you must *never* go without. It takes only a matter of minutes before the damage is done. And as dangerous as sun damage is to skin, it's nothing compared to the damage that can be done to Skin when it's unprotected, unshielded, and exposed to harmful rays.

That's about it: cleanse, tone, moisturize, and protect. It's a good plan for skin. And it's an even better plan for Skin. Will it make your Skin perfect? No. But it will make it strong, healthy, clean, nourished, and protected. That's exactly what you need in order to survive a Skin crisis.

P.S.: Going More than Skin Deep

Just in case I haven't said it clearly already, here's what I want you to know: Having a Skin crisis is a normal part of life. It's not easy or pleasant, but it's normal.

A Skin crisis can be rooted in all kinds of things — appearance, relationships, emotions, circumstances, biological changes, spirituality, and more — but ultimately, the only thing that is going to help you navigate through a Skin crisis is God and his truth. The world is a bad source of truth and guidance.

No matter what the world says, you are beautiful. As the song says, there could never be a more beautiful you. But more importantly, you are Beautiful. And you can become more and more Beautiful — both during and after your Skin crisis — if you focus on God instead of you, if you serve others instead of yourself, if you believe truth instead of the world, and if you take the time to follow a simple but important Skin care regime.

You are amazing. You are God-created, God-designed, and God-planned. You are miraculous in every way. You are an indescribable part of God's creation. You are valuable and meaningful and worthy. You are loved, adored, and cherished by God.

In fact, when God looks at you, *you take his breath away.* I can't repeat that enough.

No matter what kind of Skin crisis you are going through, do not ever, ever forget that.

Advice from the Experts

Usually experts are doctors, professors, social workers, lawyers, psychologists, politicians, or other adults who swoop in and tell you how to fix/change/survive something. But the experts you're going to read here are six young women who, just like you, went through a Skin crisis during their junior and senior high years.

Brooke Hillsmeyer, Brittany Atkinson, Amanda Sliepka, Amy Taylor, Annie Surber, Ruby Behringer, Emi Reinebold, and Kristin Parry are similar in many ways. They all volunteer in either a junior or senior high ministry. They're all in college. They all have learned how to cope with the periodic Skin crisis that still occurs in their lives. And they all love Jesus.

But they're also very different. They went to different-sized high schools. They're pursuing different college majors and have different interests. One of them is in a serious dating relationship, one is in a semi-serious dating relationship, and the others are single. They attend different churches. They are different shapes and sizes. They have different complexions, different hair color, different fashion sense, and different personalities.

For some of them, their Skin crisis started with unhappiness about appearance — most often centered around their complexion and weight. One girl was so embarrassed by her weight that she always stood with her arms crossed in front of her to hide herself from people's gazes. A few years later, when she understood more about health and nutrition, she decided to cut junk food and sugary drinks from her diet and she eventually slimmed down — without doing anything insane or obsessive. She's now very comfortable with her size (10) and doesn't care if it fits the world's ideal or not.

A few of the girls felt enormous amounts of pressure from their moms to be thin. There were lots of backhanded comments that were hurtful, which resulted in an eating disorder for one and severe unhappiness for another. Those issues haven't totally disappeared, but over time, both of them have learned how to be content with their bodies, just as they are.

For a few of the girls, the Skin crisis had to do with being a tomboy and making the transition into adolescence, with all of its biological and body-shape changes. The trauma of shopping for bras the first time just about sent two of the girls over the edge. They wanted to be shapeless, athletic, boyish, non-feminine girls their whole lives. But nature had a different plan. It took several years, and lots of tears and trauma, but they are finally content with who they are. They can wear running shorts and T-shirts one day and feel okay, and can wear a bridesmaid dress and heels the next day and feel okay too (though they're pretty happy once they get out of the dress and heels and back into comfortable clothes).

Some of the girls went through a Skin crisis because they were quiet, shy, introverted girls who didn't have the confidence to step out of their shell and try new things like they wanted. But over time, they gained the confidence to move outside their comfort zone and expand their activities to include things they never thought they'd have the courage to try. In the process, they met new people, learned more about themselves, and got a better understanding of what it means to be comfortable in one's own skin and Skin.

All of these young women are strong, independent, godly, courageous ... and fun. They are wonderful role models. They have a confidence that isn't self-centered or proud. But even with all the strength and independence and godliness and courage, they still deal with their own Skin crises now and then. Graduating from high school didn't magically make them Skin-crisis-proof. The main difference is that now they can face a Skin crisis head on with the strength and wisdom they've gained from experience and with the maturity and grace they've gained from being a few years older. So even though these young women are experts, that doesn't mean they have it all figured out or that they have perfect lives or that they never wish things were different.

I asked these six girls a few questions about how to deal with a Skin crisis. Here's what they — the real authorities — had to say:

What piece of advice would you give to girls to help them navigate and survive a Skin crisis?

BA: Never let a Skin crisis prevent you from trying something new or doing something you enjoy. There were so many times I wish I would have done things, but I passed on them because I was worried and self-conscious about how I would look and what people would think of me. No matter how you feel about yourself and how uncomfortable you think you'll be, stand up for what you believe in and try new things. Also, let your friends and family help you. There are people who love you and would love to help you get through any crises you face. Don't push them away.

BH: In terms of guys and a Skin crisis, I think that high school and middle school are times that should be spent with your girlfriends, having a blast with them, being girls. It's okay to have guy friends to hang out with too, but be sure to keep it balanced and sane. You'll always wish you'd had stronger girl relationships when you look back. And if you do have a boyfriend, don't turn into a recluse who never hangs out with anyone else. Ten bucks says your friends probably miss you!

AS: When you sense a panicky feeling starting in your gut and moving into your head, remember to stop and breathe. You may not have control over what others say about you or do to you, but you do have control over your reaction. Stop. Breathe.

RB: Even though it may feel like a Skin crisis is the only thing going on in your life right now, it isn't. It comforted me to remember that I had the rest of my life to figure stuff out and that this was only one scene in the long movie of my life. There are many more important things to fret about, but I also know that being confident in yourself *is* important — so remember: If the creator made you, then that is how he wanted you to be. He loves you just the way you are.

AT: I wish someone would have told me this — remember how temporary high school is. Had I known then that I wouldn't care what others thought, or liked or disliked about me, just a few years later (now), I would have done a lot of things different. High school is not the be-all and end-all. Don't let your world revolve around trying to satisfy yourself through the approval of others — eventually, you'll realize how trivial that really is.

KP: My family is British — we enjoy humor. The very best piece of advice I could give to any girl — and it's one of the main things that got me through high school — is learn to laugh at yourself. I did a lot of laughing, even while I was crying, in order to survive high school and all the crises and drama. And another thing: be countercultural. Be someone who makes other girls feel beautiful and cared for instead of pointing out their "flaws" or weaknesses.

ER: Best advice ever — don't take yourself too seriously. Next best piece of advice — don't compare yourself to others. Someone told me that comparison is the thief of joy. Also (and I wish someone had told me this) you're not crazy and your feelings are valid. There are so many difficult things to go through in junior and senior high, and sometimes adults will tell you to just get over it or stop being so emotional, or whatever. Sometimes maybe you do need to get a grip, but you're not crazy, and your feelings are real.

What kinds of Skin crises do you still struggle with now that you're out of high school?

BA: I sometimes still struggle with self-esteem issues, but never as bad as when I was a teenager. I also sometimes worry about things like getting a job, career choices, where I'm going to live, and whether or not I'll get married — typical college-aged stuff.

AS: Even though I know it's not true, I sometimes still have moments where I don't feel skinny enough or pretty enough. But I've learned that this is a pretty common struggle for lots of women, so I've been able to put it in perspective and keep myself from getting dragged down by it.

AT: I still find myself sometimes absorbing and believing lies from the media and other people. That pressure never really goes away totally. And I sometimes still struggle with wanting to find approval and acceptance from the world and the people in it.

RB: The pressure from the media, and the lie that I'm not good enough or I'm not worthy because of my body, still gets to me sometimes.

AS: If I start looking too far ahead into my future, I get twitchy and nervous because, as a planner, I like to know what's coming. When I don't take the time to relax and discern what's really going on, I can get into a panic. But I'm way better at this than I used to be.

KP: Right now, I'm single and very content with that. But a lot of my friends are either in serious relationships or engaged or recently married, and people keep asking me about that and even making comments about it. Even though I'm not looking for a serious relationship right now, I sometimes find myself having a crisis about it simply because of other people's opinions and influence.

What things do you do when you find yourself on the brink of a crisis?

BA: First off, I admit that I'm having a crisis or that I'm struggling with something. Then I immediately pray and talk about it with a friend I trust. That's probably the biggest difference between now and high school — I'm better able to sense what's going on around me and inside me, so I can be more proactive about dealing with it right away.

AT: I read the Bible and talk to God. I've realized that I can't hide from God, so when life gets too hard, or I find myself caught up in the wrong things, I just hand it all over to him right away. Sometimes it feels like I'm going to explode from the pressures of life, but I know God never gives me more than I can handle with his help. It also helps me to look back on prior trials I've gone through to see how God has worked. It reminds me that he's always there and that I can trust him.

AS: I breathe deeply. I exhale. I remind myself that God made me *exactly* how he wants me to be. Being more aware of that now has helped me see how ridiculous some of my high school issues were in the greater scheme of life. I focus on the fact that God has a plan laid out for me, instead of getting caught up in how I'm supposed to look or how I'm supposed to "perform."

RB: I pray. And I try to avoid having crisis moments in the first place by avoiding almost every magazine out there. They don't help me feel good about myself, so the smartest thing is to not read or look at them. I read books that help me to become the kind of woman God wants me to be. And I try to surround myself with encouraging and loving people.

KP: When I feel a crisis coming on — and even before then — I seek wisdom from people in the next stage of life, people who I admire and trust and who love God. They've been where I am and they've gone through the things I'm going through. They give much better advice and counsel than any magazine or talk show ever could.

Here's what I hope you hear these young women saying:

- life doesn't automatically get easy after high school
- having crises about appearance, friends, future, etc. is part of life
- the world's lies and pressures are still there, even for adults
- life experience and added wisdom makes it easier to cope with crises
- being aware of and prepared for crisis moments is key to surviving them
- prayer, God's truth, and good Christian friends are the best sources of comfort and advice, especially when the issue is Skin deep

Brooke, Brittany, Amy, Annie, Amanda, Ruby, Emi, and Kristin have learned how to be comfortable in their own skin, and how to celebrate their own Skin. It wasn't easy. It wasn't quick. And it wasn't painless. But they made it to the next stage of life. You will too. I really believe that . . . not because you yourself are awesome, fabulous, perfect, amazing, stupendous, (and every other over-the-top word), but because you have an awesome, fabulous, perfect, amazing, stupendous (and every other over-the-top word) God who loves you and cares about you.

So go ahead . . . live a life that's more than skin deep, and instead goes Skin deep. He'd want you to!

Bibliography

Brinton, D.G, MD and G.H. Nampheys, MD. *Personal Beauty* (originally called *Health and the Human Form*, 1860). Facsimile edition. Bedford, MA: Applewood Books, 1994.

Hustad, Alice M. *Strictly Confidential*. Minneapolis: Augsburg, 1944.

Kise, Jane and Kevin Johnson. *Find Your Fit*. Minneapolis: Bethany House, 1998.

Moxcey, Mary E. *Girlhood and Character*. New York: Abingdon Press, 1916.

Warner, Mabel Hale. *Beautiful Girlhood*. Anderson, IN: Warner Press, 1922.

Wood-Allen, Mary, MD. *What a Young Woman Ought to Know*. Philadelphia: Vir Publishing, 1898.

Talk It Up!

Want free books?
First looks at the best new fiction?
Awesome exclusive merchandise?

We want to hear from you!

Give us your opinions on titles, covers, and stories.
Join the Z Street Team.

Email us at zstreetteam@zondervan.com
to sign up today!

Also—Friend us on Facebook!

www.facebook.com/goodteenreads

- Video Trailers
- Connect with your favorite authors
- Sneak peeks at new releases
- Giveaways
- Fun discussions
- And much more!